Could **you** take a photo like this?

Overthinking may be what's stopping you

Learn to act at the non-conscious level to transform your practice

THE
**MASTER
PHOTOGRAPHER**
THE JOURNEY FROM
GOOD TO GREAT
REVISED EDITION

BOB RYAN

THE MASTER PHOTOGRAPHER

THE JOURNEY FROM GOOD TO GREAT

Bob Ryan

Bourchier Books

Published by
Bourchier Books
Gable House, 46 High Street,
Malmesbury, SN16 9AT, UK

www.bourchierbooks.com

First edition published in 2016
© Bob Ryan and Andy Beel

This 2017 edition © Bob Ryan

The author wishes to thank Andy Beel and Alison Price for granting
permission to use some of their photographs in this book, and Andy
Beel for his text contributions in Chapters 6 and 7.

British Library Cataloguing in Publication Data
Data available

Library of Congress Cataloging in Publication Data
Data available

Typeset by Red Axe Design

Printed in Great Britain by Short Run Press Ltd., UK

ISBN 978-0-9934692-7-5

CONTENTS

PREFACE TO THE
REVISED EDITION

Writing the first edition of *The Master Photographer* was a huge challenge: how to integrate psychology, learning theory and photography in a way that would help the 'good' photographer make a real difference in the development of their art. This new edition is the next stage as we reach out to an international audience.

The difficulty with any new edition is deciding what to include and what to leave out. In the end, some simple decisions were made: we would add more of Alison Price's gorgeous photography to the book. Andy Beel's superb images still grace the pages of this edition and his contributions on tonality in monochrome work and the application of the learning principles developed in the book to the problems of creativity have been invaluable and inspiring.

Further developments in my research at the University of Gloucestershire and inspired by the first edition have also borne fruit. The structure of expertise described in Chapters 3 and 4 initially was developed from the published output of numerous photographic societies. Two questions still needed to be answered: first, was that structure of expertise meaningful to those who put their eye to a viewfinder and to those who view the result and, second, was the hierarchy we placed upon them representative of the way skilled photographers view them? Studies using the output of the IMP Test has given a clear answer: yes, in both cases.

Finally, some acknowledgements: first to Andy and Alison for the contributions they have made to this book and for their critical support as the text took shape. Second, I would like to thank my son Dr Joe Ryan, whose outstanding expertise as a clinical psychologist has helped me clarify many of the issues that this book raises about the workings of the photographer's mind. Third, I would like to give a special thanks to three superb photographers who have both inspired and challenged my work: Chris Weston, Rod Wainwright and Peter Phillips. And finally, the publishing team at Bourchier led by the ever-patient Elizabeth Stone. All sins of course, whether of omission or commission, are down to me.

The Maiden in the Falls
— Bob Ryan, 2015

INTRODUCTION

'In this book I train you how to forget. Not to forget in the sense of not being able to remember what you know, but forgetting in the sense of not needing to remember what you know. You just know.'

– Bob Ryan

In this chapter we look at the way people think: the rational way and the intuitive way. Although we are taught to trust the former and often to disregard the latter, intuition can be very powerful when it is supported by expert skills and knowledge. In photography much of our image-making works at a non-conscious level and here we start you on the journey that will help you to exploit your intuitive power and make the jump from good to great.

I give you a promise. A promise backed up by 40 years of research in the psychology of learning and judgement – research that has the potential to take your photography to a new level of excellence. I will show you an approach to developing your skills that is systematic, thorough and, in photographic terms, revolutionary. What you do with your photography then is up to you: you may sell your work, exhibit it or just enjoy it; but, whatever you do, I believe you will regard this book as the best investment you have made on your photographic journey.

As you progress along the path we describe you will discover:

1. A new level of excellence and mastery in your image taking.

2. A heightened sense of discovery and satisfaction in the process of the deep learning our method entails.

3. Your full expressive and creative abilities, which will emerge as you train your skills in intuitive thinking.

4. That much of the photography you found difficult will become active at a non-conscious level and, as a result, you will be able to make key photographic judgements quickly and effectively.

5. You will gain a new sense of freedom in your photography. In your mastery of the medium you will be able to express your intent with imagination and creativity.

6. That the separation in your mind between your subject, your camera and you will dissolve and you will become one with them.

Photography, at its most satisfying best, is a deeply intuitive art. When we search for the creative moment we engage in a thought process that is non-conscious, rapid and, when we get it right, effortless. It is in this non-conscious moment of appreciation and action that our image creation skills are activated. This book is about the deep skilling of your non-conscious, photographic brain and how you can elevate its potential to a point that your full expression can be realized.

Many of you reading this book will be well versed in some of the technical issues discussed. Indeed, there are many wonderful books demonstrating what you need to know in photography and I list a few I think are among the best at the end of this book. However, they all miss one crucial issue – it's not 'what' but 'how' you know that matters. We are all extremely good at learning 'stuff'. For example, fortunes have been made selling cookery books, but none of them tells you how to become a great chef. Money has been made selling great photography books, but until now none tell you how to become a great photographer. Photography, like cookery, is not an additive skill – it requires a different way of acquiring skill and then using it.

The difference between this book and the rest is that we will show you how to 'hardwire' the technical expertise you need to know into your non-conscious patterns of thought. We will show you how to use a powerful, fast and reliable mode of thinking we all have at our disposal but in the modern world have been educated to ignore. Once trained you will find that your photographic ability has gone through a step change, freeing your mind so that you can realize your creative and expressive best.

This chapter explores the basics of our approach and the way that we think about photography. It presents the crucial concepts that support our method – the rest of the book will not make much sense without understanding them. Chapter 2 introduces three key principles that will accelerate your photographic journey – they are easy to remember but you will need dedicated effort to put them into practice. The following chapters then work through our process, initially giving you some easy gains but then go on to the most challenging and ultimately rewarding elements of our method.

SOME WORDS OF CAUTION:

Caution 1: This is not an 'easy' guide to being a great photographer. Books or teachers who promise that are purveyors of the photographic equivalent of 'snake oil'. What we offer is the most efficient means of achieving excellence and how you can avoid the pitfalls in building expertise. It still entails hard work and committed practice. If the thought of that is not exciting, then basket weaving may be more to your taste.

Caution 2: We do assume some essential competency in the use of your camera. So if you have just purchased the latest Nikon, Fuji or Canon and haven't got a clue how to use it then you are not quite ready for this book. But, to help you, the skills we assume are shown in the appendix, so practise them on your new camera – don't worry about the quality of the images you take, just practise the essential camera-handling skills until you know where everything is without fumbling.

Caution 3: If you are an experienced photographer you may find your photography deteriorates before it improves. This is a common outcome when surrendering one mode of thinking and embracing another. Much boils down to trust and if you are already happy with your image making, then read no further. On the other hand if, like so many photographers, you feel that you have hit your creative and expressive ceiling, and do not know how to push the boundaries of your art, then this book is for you.

Caution 4: The conventional methods of teaching photography are useful to a point, but no further. Even great photographers do not tell you what they actually do, they tell you what they think they do. So, read the manuals for your camera by all means, read books that tell you how to do tricky bits of post-processing, also read books that explore why some images really work and others don't. There is a great list of such titles at the end of the book. However, be very sceptical of any book that claims to tell you how to become 'creative' or how to acquire a 'photographer's eye' – they are well meant but, as we will see later, may achieve exactly the opposite result.

Exhibit 1.1

Henry

– Bob Ryan, 2006

He's a dog, but how does he know things before we do? It's because he has become very adept at using 'cue-dependent memory'

It isn't often that a book on photography gets down to business starting with a cute image of a puppy – in this case called Henry. There is a reason. To understand the 'photographic moment' we need to appreciate a little of the psychology that drives our own thinking process, and to help understand that let's think about cats and dogs. 'Be more dog' was a catchphrase used in a series of O2 adverts that left viewers both amused by the antics of a cat being urged to 'be more dog' and bemused by what it meant. One interpretation, whether or not intended by the advertisers, is that dogs have a way of thinking that cats (and perhaps we) should emulate.

Dogs, as any dog owner will recognize, are deeply intuitive and emotional animals and it is their emotional responsiveness that drives their intuition. They have the ability to pick up and act upon subtle cues from our behaviour and other aspects of their environment. Dogs have an enhanced ability to associate cause and effect very rapidly. So, when a dog perceives the tiny cues in the changing behaviour of people around them – cues that the humans involved might not be aware of – it knows that its master or mistress is on their way home. It's not clairvoyance; it is simply that they have been optimized by evolution to exploit one style of thinking to the full – a style that utilizes cue-dependent memory. We call this type of thinking 'intuition'.[1] In this way they can exploit their niche in the animal order as pack, opportunistic scavengers, and in this they have a different way of thinking from cats.

Now, neither cats nor dogs have the thinking power of a human being. But perhaps the urge to 'be more dog' is one to be more intuitive – to open up our intuition and to surrender some of our dependency on the rational thinking to which our massive brains are so adept and to which we have become progressively 'enculturated' – particularly in the Western world.

But why is intuitive thinking so important in photography? Why should we become more dog? The answer is this: intuitive thinking really is effortless, it operates below our conscious level of reasoning, it is extraordinarily fast, it is surprisingly accurate and reliable when developed in the right way and, crucially, the engine that drives it is emotional intensity. It comes from the gut – or if you prefer it, from the heart – and if we develop it properly it has the power to transform our photography from the mechanical and the mundane to the purest expression of the human spirit.

When you pick up your camera and look at a potential scene through the viewfinder you will find yourself getting drawn into a range of different mental activities. The frontal lobe of your brain is in overdrive. You look at the scene isolating your point of focus and the appropriate exposure, shutter speed and ISO setting to achieve the image you want. You will reposition the camera's field of view to eliminate unwanted elements in the background and you home in on the subject, focusing on the key point of interest. You press the shutter and then chimp the back of your camera to admire what you have done.[2]

---

[1]   The *Oxford English Dictionary* defines intuition as an ability to understand or know something based upon feelings rather than facts. Tilmann Betsch, in his book, Plessner, H., Betsch, C., and Betsch, T., *Intuition in Judgment and Decision Making* (Routledge, 2014), defines intuition as 'a process of thinking'. 'The input to this process is mostly provided by knowledge stored in long term memory that has been primarily acquired via associative learning. The input is processed automatically and without conscious awareness. The output of the process is a feeling that can serve as a basis for judgment and decisions' (p. 4).

[2]   Chimping is the process of looking at an image on the back of a camera. Why 'chimping'? It is because photographers get excited by what they see and go 'oo, oo' in a chimp sort of way.

The result may be OK; the histogram may be a bit too far to the right, so you retake the shot, or it may be that your overall feeling is one of disappointment. The camera has not recorded what you saw. So what went wrong?

The answer is that what originally fired your excitement was a product of your untrained intuition. You responded emotionally to what you saw, you recognized the potential for an image, it happened in a blink of your eye. You then tried to reconstruct that emotional response in the way that we have all been taught – the rational way, the way driven into us by our educational system and our culture. As you did so that moment of intuitive insight evaporated. Your initial intuition may have been flawed for reasons we will examine shortly, or it may have been good but it was then paralysed by analysis.

How would you like to come up with images that are gloriously evocative, perfectly executed and use light and colour to brilliant effect? The great English painter Turner was not a photographer but he was a master of colour and light. His grandson, as a young child, watched him paint The Fighting Temeraire. *This painting of a great warship, bathed in the light of early morning, is a masterpiece of stunning beauty. His grandson recalled how Turner very quickly smothered the canvas in raw paint of different hues and intensities. Then, with his fingers and brushes, he started to push and mould the pigments on the canvas and before the boy's astonished eyes the great ship began to emerge just as it would have done on the water, on that morning in Turner's imagination, in the blazing glory of the rising sun. Turner was displaying his skill as an artist driven by a deep, intuitive understanding of the methods and the potential of his art.*

NOW THE PROBLEM

Intuition is a hugely powerful mode of thinking. Often it is vital for our survival. Daniel Kahneman, a Nobel Prize-winning cognitive psychologist, relates an event that perfectly demonstrates the power of intuition.[3] A fire chief led his men into a blaze that was located in the kitchen of a house. This is the place where most domestic fires catch hold. On entering the room he and his men, in their protective gear, were confronted by an inferno of smoke and fire. He immediately ordered his men out without attempting to subdue the blaze.

---

[3]   D. Kahneman, *Thinking Fast and Thinking Slow* (Harmondsworth: Penguin, 2012).

Within seconds the kitchen floor collapsed – the fire had started in the basement, not in the kitchen.

How had he recognized the danger? In his debrief he recollected hearing tiny sounds that an inexperienced firefighter might have ignored. He did not, when he went into the kitchen, reason it out – he did not use what psychologists refer to as 'System 2 thinking'. His brain, effortlessly and instantly, brought together what he saw, his experience and his skill, and he knew intuitively what he had to do. This is intuitive, or 'System 1 thinking', at its best. But there is an important point here: the quality of his experience was crucial – he had many years of intensive training and experience behind him. He had seen it all.

Exhibit 1.2
Joseph Mallord William Turner,
The Fighting Temeraire
© The National Gallery, London.
Turner Bequest, 1856

Dual processing models of reasoning distinguish between two modes of thinking:

System 1 thinking is the name given to the non-conscious mode of thinking we call 'intuition'. Intuition is driven by what is known as 'cue-dependent memory' or memories embedded and reinforced by repeated exposure to the situation or problem. Intense emotional experiences boost this non-conscious learning process.

System 2 thinking is the reasoning we undertake at a conscious level – it entails logical analysis of a problem, the rational ordering of a plan of action and then a decision based upon the results of what can be intense and lengthy mental activity.

Exhibit 1.3
Biet Georgius – Lalibela, Ethiopia
– Andy Beel, 2006
This image won Andy first place at the London Salon. Like many of his images, he cannot recollect what inspired him to take the shot. He just did

Another important element of this story is that when the fire chief went into the blazing building his attention was 'hyper-alert' – he would have been very professional and controlled in his behaviour but he was emotionally engaged. He was 'in the moment' and he almost certainly felt the sort of fear that good stage performers experience – the sort of 'fear' that opens the brain to a higher order judgement.

So, in order to engage our intuitive mind, we need:

1. **A deep and wide knowledge of the subject.**

2. **Deep practice.**

3. **To be emotionally engaged with the subject.**

4. **Believe in what we are doing – to have faith in the process.**

5. **To free our mind and fully enter the moment.**

With these five elements in place the subject, our camera, our mind and our body become integrated – they become one.

There is no need to hold down the shutter and hope we catch the moment. Just one shot is all it takes. It happened for Alison Price when she took her prize-winning image of an orang-utan and its dying child.

Alison's tale:

Alison trained as a 'scene of crime' photographer and in the period of her work with the police saw many things she found deeply upsetting. Although the camera was, to a small extent, a barrier to the horror of what she saw, she was learning her photography under great emotional stress. Like war photographers, she learnt her camera craft in the field. And, like many who learn their craft that way, the camera became a cue, a reminder of what she had seen, and although for twenty years after her police work she did little photography, when her love of wildlife and her skill in photography came together again she was able to take the image shown in Exhibit 1.4.

How did she achieve this ability? How could she, taking up a digital camera so many years later, activate the necessary skills to get a shot like this? Is there a secret? Yes there is, but unless you are forced to take your camera into highly stressful and sometimes terrifying situations, it will take work. You cannot cheat. There is no magic formula but there are ways that the process of achieving excellence in photography can be made more rapid and productive. So, if you want to take images that express your 'voice or vision' in the way you intend, that allows you to express your feelings and creativity clearly with conviction, then this is where you start.

In the next chapter we explore the process by which you can develop your intuitive photographic ability through our 'EPF' method – an approach that combines emotional intensity, deep practice and feedback into a powerful learning experience. The chapters that follow will help you learn about your own photographic abilities and how you can develop them to the point that you don't need to think about them, you just act upon them.

Exhibit 1.4
Mother and Child , Sepilok
Sanctuary, Malaysia
– Alison Price, 2010
Alison was watching this sad scene in an open sanctuary for orang-utans in Malaysia. She made the emotional connection and took the shot

2
THE EPF METHOD

'We choose to go to the moon in this decade and do the other things, not because they are easy, but because they are hard.'

– J.F. Kennedy, September 1962

In this chapter we explore a method of learning that helps 'burn-in' the skills and knowledge you require to make the rapid judgements photography demands. This is our EPF method where E is for emotional engagement, P is for deep practice and F is for feedback. Our method is challenging but is designed to help you accelerate your learning at the non-conscious, intuitive level.

THE EPF METHOD

When Alison took her image of the orang-utan what do you think was going through her mind? Optimal exposure? Focus? Depth of field? Or did she just have the camera in her hand and take the shot? Did she 'pre-visualize' the moment or was this a spontaneous reaction to the sadness she could see and the desperate condition of the baby? Was she reacting with the cool detachment of an accountant examining the financial affairs of a local firm? Or was she emotionally engaged too? She knew that the maternal instinct of the orang-utan is one of the deepest in the animal kingdom. She had seen tragedy and death in her work as a scene of crime photographer. She had become deeply practised in her art, and in the instant when she pressed the shutter what happened in her brain was what happened in the brain of the fire chief. Multiple streams of thought, deep channels of experience and a high degree of technical skill were brought together.

Emotion

So, what are the key elements that we recognize here? The first is emotion – you need to feel some kind of emotional attraction or engagement with the subject. If a potential image does nothing for you then don't press the shutter. If it does nothing for you then it will do nothing for anyone else. Emotion is your autonomic response to certain moods: it is about your intensity of feeling when confronted with events or things that excite you.

Fear is an emotional response to danger, anger to challenge, elation to achievement and so on. Emotional intensity is the strength of the feeling you experience and in photography it has two important functions: if we can communicate the intensity we feel through our images then they will have impact. The second is that the more intense the emotion we attach to an event or an action the more we remember it. At one extreme, we can see the product of this in men and women who have experienced great horror or shock. All the physical, visual and auditory cues become embedded in a traumatized instant and are painfully absorbed. For some, any of the associated cues stimulate a painful reliving of the whole experience – a process the rational mind cannot control. We call this 'post-traumatic stress disorder' or PTSD.[1]

We do not advocate enhancing your learning by seeking out violent or horrific events to photograph. However, by building emotional intensity the input-processing of skills and thoughts can be enhanced. In the chapters that follow I will show you ways that this can be effectively (and safely) achieved.

So, to energize and embed our learning we need to energize the learning experience through emotional engagement. This is the 'E' of the EPF method.

Practice

The second element we can gather from the experience of Alison and so many other great photographers is practice. One great myth is that talent is born – all the evidence collected in many different areas is that it is commitment and practice that make the difference, lots of it. A common estimate suggests that at least 10,000 hours of consistent practice is required to bring about the degree of expertise needed to drive high levels of intuitive skill. But there is practice and there is deep practice. Most photographers practise by doing, getting out with their camera and pressing the shutter. Deep practice is where practice is constructed that makes the application of the desired

---

[1] The results of PTSD are to be seen in people who has suffered deep and painful trauma. Many deal with the aftermath of horror successfully but, for a significant number, what results is a condition that requires understanding and treatment. A good and accessible insight can be found in A. Ehlers and D. M. Clarke, A Cognitive Model of Posttraumatic Stress Disorder, *Behaviour Research and Therapy* 38 (2000), 319–45.

skill intensely challenging. It is the exercise of deep practice that builds intuitive ability and will give you that special edge.[2]

To be effective each learning stage has to be just at the edge of your current capability. For example, musicians achieve mastery of the score by slowly practising a complex sequence of notes over and over again until each sequence becomes embedded in memory. Then, once each sequence has been perfected, they are slowly combined until the piece is mastered as whole. Children in Brazil learn their football in a small training room where the onus is on speed, ball control and accuracy in passing the ball from one team member to another within a tightly constrained space. After years of practice they emerge to the senior game where the open spaces of a full pitch allow them to exploit the skills developed in the 'Futsal' or *Futebol de Salao*.

The characteristics of deep practice can be summarized as follows:

1. **The practice must be structured** – we achieve that through the definition of ten photographic constructs, which each taken individually or as a whole represent the skills and knowledge required to become a master photographer.

2. **The practice must be demanding** – we show you ways to make your practice challenging but ultimately rewarding. As we noted above, it has to be at the limit of your capabilities such that there is a good chance you will fail to achieve what you intend with your practice.

3. **The practice must be repetitive** – we show you how to direct your efforts so that every practice session allows you to consolidate your learning.

4. **The practice must be separable** – what this means is you need to focus on each of the skills separately. Spend time working on focus for example, forget the rest – just focus on focus.

5. **The practice must be open to feedback** – your practice must be such that you can rapidly assess your performance as you proceed.

---

2   K. Anders Eriksson, *The Road to Excellence: The Acquisition of Expert Performance in the Arts and Sciences, Sports and Games* (New York: Psychology Press, 2014). This is an excellent book of readings first compiled in 1996 examining the development of expertise and the role of practice.

So, the second element of the EPF method is the application of deep practice to photography. Deep practice is practice that takes you to the limits of your capability and where failure to achieve frequently occurs.

Feedback

The third element of the EPF method is crucial and it is feedback. Where deep practice is supported by rapid and constructive feedback, errors are recognized and corrected, and as a consequence the rate of learning is multiplied. You should check your performance, rigorously correcting your mistakes as you proceed. Never leave a mistake behind, pick up on it, cherish it – it is a thing to be welcomed. By failing we learn.

In one very important respect, digital photography has brought with it a rapid mechanism for feedback and that is the camera's rear monitor. In an instant we can check exposure along with focus and composition. Within a few minutes our images can be downloaded onto a computer and a more detailed assessment made. The technology closes the loop of learning and helps us bind and encode the skills into our intuitive behaviour, providing we use the feedback consistently and productively.

The other good source of feedback is from a friendly but critical coach or tutor. Seek out people who will give you constructive but critical advice. Don't look for advice from those who are just nice, don't look for support from those who tell you what a great photographer you are. As the EPF method takes root in your thinking and practice you will soon recognize those who really know what they are talking about and can help you on your way.

Constructively used, feedback is, therefore, the third element of the EPF method of building intuitive skill in photography. Feedback allows you to confirm the success of your learning and transforms acquired skills into automatic responses to specified situations.

The three elements of the EPF method – emotional intensity, deep practice and feedback – are designed to build your intuitive skill. They are the means by which we invite you to train the non-conscious processes that allow you to combine the many different variables that go into the creation of an image that connects you to the subject and you to your viewer.

Well, that all sounds very straightforward. What can go wrong? The answer is that you may well have learnt a patchwork of skills that are incomplete. Most reasonably competent photographers know the 'rule of thirds' and the elements of exposure. They know how to focus their camera and have a reasonable idea of the concept of 'depth of field'. What is more problematic is that when they are taught by a genuinely skilled and intuitive photographer, the person concerned will teach them the System 2 approach to photography. They are *ex post* rationalizing their experience. Here are two stories of two very successful professional photographers with long experience in their respective genres. They had both, after many years of work and effort, produced wonderful work, but when attempting to teach photography both fell into the trap of reinforcing System 2 approaches to their art.

Sian

Sian is a very experienced and successful photographer who has built a business in stage and music photography. Naturally, the biggest problem she confronts in her work is working with low and strongly contrasting light. She also runs photographic short courses and she places great emphasis on 'getting the exposure right'. Her evening talks are engaging discussions of the theory of exposure – balancing ISO, shutter speed and aperture. When appraising the images of the course members she critiques the histogram – too far to the left, too far to the right and so on. She has rationalized the challenges of her particular genre; but, without disputing the importance of correct exposure, can you see the problem she was inadvertently creating? She is overstressing the role of exposure in image making and enforcing a preoccupation with a technical issue out of context. She is boosting rational System 2 thinking.

Adam

Adam is a wildlife photographer whose image making was highly creative and original in capturing animal behaviour. He is able to create moments of connection that draw the viewer into the animal's world. He, like Sian, has an urge to teach and in his evening critique sessions he focuses, with his students, on the elements of composition: shape, line, texture and so forth. He also emphasizes the practice of 'pre-visualization' – the notion that a successful image-maker needs to think out and construct the image in their head before they go out to take the shot. Indeed, he is convinced that images are a product of the mind rather than of the external world. In philosophical terms he is a 'rationalist', a tradition of thought that goes back to the time of the great Greek philosophers Socrates and Plato. The problem with this is that Adam is concentrating attention on the construction of the image by visualizing and setting the scene. But even Adam is beginning to wonder what is missing and is struggling to find his inner voice.

Few teachers know the techniques of enabling intuitive skill in their students – like Sian and Adam they lapse into the language and logic of rational System 2 thinking.[3] The injunction to pre-visualize the image is an invitation to engage in rational, System 2 photography. It is an invitation to abandon creativity in the moment and to play out your preconceptions, biases and misconceptions in your image making. Obviously, we all proceed with some idea of the subject of our photography – that is what we call photographic 'intent'. What we do not know and cannot guess is how nature and the world will present itself to us.

There is no doubt that a rational and evaluative approach to photography will take you a long way. It can be developed through the conventional approaches to learning. To be effective this type of learning needs to be free from emotional pressure and it is this habituation to 'emotion-free learning' that drives much teaching practice in schools and universities and, incidentally, motivates the reductionist process in the natural sciences. Now the bad news: following our approach to learning you may get worse before you get better. This will be only a temporary phase, but I think it only fair to warn you it may happen.[4]

To open up the possibility of much higher levels of performance you need to build System 1 thinking. But to develop an intuitive understanding of image making you must first disentangle yourself from the conventional approach to photography and through a process akin to intellectual *ju-jitsu* turn it against itself and start the painful, but intensely rewarding, process of unlearning and rebuilding your photographic intuition using the most powerful emotional drivers you can.

---

[3] The Western approach to education is through training in 'System 2' thinking and what is often described as 'learning by rote' is regarded as – at best – old-fashioned. In the Eastern educational systems learning by rote still has a big place in the curriculum – it is recognized that if properly constructed the learning that results is deeply embedded and will become intuitive knowledge. Ask the typical Western child what is 7 times 8 and you will have to wait a moment or two whilst they search their memory for the answer. Ask a Chinese child and the answer – 56 – will be immediately fired back.

[4] There is good research evidence that 'rational thinking' can hinder the effective and efficient use of intuition. N. Ambady, The Perils of Pondering: Intuition and Thin Slice Judgments, *Psychological Inquiry* 21:4 (2010), 271–8, provides a very useful analysis of this issue. Ambady quotes that famous line from Shakespeare's *Julius Caesar* where Caesar is commenting on Cassius's mean and hungry look: 'He thinks too much; such men are dangerous.'

BUILDING EMOTIONAL INTENSITY

Great learning does not come through the recitation of theories and facts – it comes through telling stories. In the Bible, Christ taught his message through parables, Aesop taught his lessons through fables and Shakespeare searched the depths of the human condition through his plays and poetry. Through stories we learn the important lessons of life. Why? Because stories engage our emotions – we visualize the problem and our mind internalizes and associates the emotion with the message the story relates.

All great teachers love telling stories – they tread a fine line between what is truth and what is fiction and, using a situation which plucks at our sympathy or gently knocks our funny bone, reveal a higher truth and, as a result, they get their message across in an unforgettable way. That is why we tell you stories like those of Sian and Adam. You will also find telling yourself stories about the image you are about to take can be very helpful when building your emotional connection to the subject concerned.

So, in developing our photographic intuition, we need to enhance the emotional intensity of our learning experience. There are a number of ways of doing this and I will suggest a number of strategies for you to try. However, they all follow a common path. First, the chosen method needs to disentangle you from your everyday concerns. It needs to quieten the 'chattering monkeys' that constitute the rational-thinking mind and push back on your everyday concerns and anxieties. For some, this quietening process is as simple as getting away from home for an hour or two or indeed a day or two. For others it is through the practice of a simple meditative technique like 'mindfulness' or perhaps just sitting quietly and reflecting on the good things in life. These few moments are very important before starting your practice.

Whatever method you choose, you need to bring yourself 'to the moment' in order to prepare yourself for the next step of enhancing your emotional state. There are two excellent steps that will help you. First, try to activate a particularly intense memory associated with the subject of your image making. When looking at birds flying in to a local wildlife centre, I like to think of the film *Where Eagles Dare* and the hugely evocative music during its opening credits. I tell myself stories about the waterbirds flying in from their 2,000-mile migration with weary wings outstretched and feet and flight feathers down as, at long last, they approach their home water. I know that humming the theme-tune from the movie is a bit daft, but as the men in white coats with the straitjacket close in, I get the shot I dream of before making my escape. Building a 'narrative' around what you intend to shoot is a powerful priming strategy.

The second element to the emotional priming of your learning is by playing over your earphones music that has a strong emotionally elevating effect for you. Tastes in music differ wildly but for me something like Denez Prigent's 'Gortoz a Ran' or perhaps 'Brothers in Arms' by Dire Straits will do the trick. So, before and whilst holding my camera to my eye to explore a scene I will play some music. Likewise, when post-processing my images I will play music in the background. It doesn't have to be sophisticated – it just has to do the trick for me.

It sounds corny, I know – but try it. I do it when setting about judging a series of images for a local camera club. I do it when I set off to take images whether I know the location or not. That burst of emotional energy is invariably enough to activate the intuitive imagination (we use that word deliberately) and then, again invariably, the image starts to reinforce – in a process I call positive feedback – the emotional intensity of the moment.

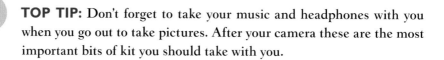

TOP TIP: Don't forget to take your music and headphones with you when you go out to take pictures. After your camera these are the most important bits of kit you should take with you.

Priming Exercise 2.1

Here is an exercise reviewing a sequence of your own images. Working with a set of images loaded into your favourite processing software go through the following steps:

1. Choose a quiet time when the worries of the world can be put to one side.

2. Relax as best you can, perhaps through some simple breathing exercises or by employing a meditative technique. Whatever does it for you – do it.

3. Put on some music that you find elevates your spirit.

4. Play your images at a pace of seven seconds each through your software's full screen mode. Don't be tempted to fiddle with them.

5. Absorb yourself in the images – let them flow.

6. Select a subset (no more than five images) that captured your imagination most strongly.

7. Work on these five images, bringing them up to a good standard by adjusting white balance, crop, exposure, clarity, etc.

8. Play the music again.

9. Review the five images – now they will be bursting into a life of their own. They will reveal their intensity to you and, with practice, in that moment your mind will become submerged in the reality of the image.

To get the best from this process avoid being critical of your images. Your mode of thought should be one of open reflection, not critical reflection – that will come later as I build your image making skills and bind them into your intuitive mental processing.

One word of warning: you may find the idea of mindfulness and particularly the use of music distracting. Why? It is because you have become habituated to rational System 2 learning where any distraction and, indeed, any distraction that engages the emotions, is a block to your learning. But persist with it. Intuitive System 1 learning is taking you another way; you are learning to associate skills and knowledge with emotions. You are 'burning them in'.

So remember – EPF: emotion, deep practice and feedback. In the next chapter we show you how to assemble your photographic skills and start to use the EPF method.

3

THE TEN PHOTOGRAPHIC COMPETENCIES

'I must be willing to give up what I am in order to become what I will be.'

– Albert Einstein

In this chapter I start by introducing you to the 'Rational Experimental Inventory', which will help you identify your preferences for both modes of thinking outlined in Chapter 1. I then take you through the construction of the photographic judgement leading to a hierarchy of constructs. These, taken as a whole, reflect the skills and expertise you need to fulfil your photographic ambition.

BURNING IN ABILITY

You may already have been taught, or have taught yourself, a wide range of photographic skills. Indeed, you may have a genre that appeals to you. You may have reached a stage of winning some competitions at the local camera club or been successful in international competitions sponsored by various photographic associations. You have possibly spent a lot on camera magazines but have become a bit weary of many of them sitting unread in the magazine rack. The problem is that you have added more software and disorganized knowledge to that already overloaded super-computer between your ears. Our task is to take those skills and 'burn' them into your brain's firmware.

To help you on your photographic way we suggest you work through a straightforward test of how receptive you are to the intuitive mode of thought that inspires great photography. To that end we recommend you download the 'Rational Experiential Inventory' (REI) from our website. It comes as a simple Excel spreadsheet where you are required to answer forty questions about yourself by placing a '1' against each question. It is important to answer the questions as carefully and honestly as you can – that way you will gain most insight from the process.

The Inventory, first developed by the psychologist Seymour Epstein,[1] is a reliable and well-validated tool for measuring your ability at either rational or intuitive thinking and the reliance you place upon either thinking mode

---

[1]   For an introduction to Epstein's work in this area see S. Epstein, Intuition from the Perspective of Cognitive-Experiential Self-Theory, in H. Plessner, C. Betsch and T. Betsch (eds), *Intuition in Judgement and Decision Making* (New York: Routledge, 2014).

in your daily life. You may find it helpful just to find out how receptive you are to the way of thinking explored in this book.

We all, to a greater or lesser degree, have some power of intuition and are capable of System 1 thinking. This can represent an extraordinarily powerful ability – although it does need to be effectively trained to the task in hand. Because intuitive System 1 thinking is not under the control of our logical/rational mind – it works too fast for that – we need to be sure that the tools it uses are appropriate for the job in hand.

TOP TIP: **Undertaking the REI inventory is easy and quick. Just go to www.bourchierbooks.com and download the inventory. It will give you an insight into how your mind works when performing tasks and solving problems. A high 'rational score' does not necessarily mean that you cannot train your intuitive thinking skills. It may take a little more time and you may become frustrated with the process. However, retaking the inventory after six months of applying the method I describe below will demonstrate the progress you are making on your journey to great photography.**

Many people are deeply mistrustful of intuition. For them the cool rational way of thinking is their preferred style – and often they are good at it. They score highly in both their rational reasoning ability and their preference for that style of solving problems. Unfortunately, if they have reached this point in this book what follows may be quite contrary to their preferred mode of thinking. Indeed, the closest they ever come to the emotional is to dismiss the concept of intuition in photography with an angry and contemptuous wave of the hand.

Roland is an exceptional wildlife photographer who created images of the 3Bs (birds, bugs and beasts) with a high degrees of precision. He insists on high technical accuracy and absolute clarity in any image he takes or judges. He does not accept portraits focusing on the expression of animals but demands that any image should show the full animal in its context. His beautifully rendered images appeared in numerous nature journals and animal encyclopaedias. When judging an image in a print competition he awarded it a score of 8 out of 15. Yet that image, which showed the intimate behaviour of animals, went on to win a major international wildlife photography competition. When asked to comment he contemptuously dismissed the winning image as 'anthropomorphic nonsense'.

The example of Roland represents a common, technical perception of certain branches of photography where no departure from realism is allowed within competitive circles. There is nothing wrong with this approach and if it is what you want from your photography then what follows will not 'tick your boxes'. However, we believe, and we hope you do too, that the route to excellence we propose will transform your ability in the performance of your art.

CONSTRUCTS AND THE POWER OF TEN

In order to understand the power of intuition you need to understand the idea of a 'construct'. Take a concept like 'exposure' in photography. When unpacking 'exposure' we realize that it is a term that covers knowledge of a number of different things we need to know:

- **the sensitivity of the sensor (ISO) and how it influences the camera's ability to capture the intensity of light;**

- **how aperture and shutter speed control the quantity of available light allowed into the camera;**

- **about the interplay between tonality and brightness and the way that the incidence of light affects the required exposure.**

In the instant of making a photographic judgement there are just too many objective and subjective variables in play – so I collapse them into a single judgement construct I term 'exposure'.

Exposure is a judgement construct and not merely a skill. It is a bigger concept than that – it represents a bundle of skills, knowledge and experience bound together in your brain and activated when the need arises. There is some evidence that with continued practice this bundle is physically reinforced by the development of a coherent cluster of neurons in the brain bound together by a white fatty substance called myelin. The more you practice the more reinforced and predictable becomes the output from this construct.[2]

---

[2] An extensive literature has developed in both psychology and medicine on the role of myelin in both brain pathologies and in learning. Myelin is a white fatty substance that protects the electrical integrity of linked neurons (the brain cells that do the processing) and appears to be strongly reinforced as a particular sequence of remembered actions are repeated. This article explains some of the science around this topic: R. Douglas Fields, White Matter in Learning, Cognition and Psychiatric Disorders, 2008, <http://www.ncbi.nlm.nih.gov/pmc/articles/PMC2486416/>.

Aha! your rational System 2 brain says 'but exposure isn't a completely distinct construct from (say) use of light' – which, as we will see, is a separate judgement construct. No, it isn't: there is a degree of overlap between most if not all the judgement constructs that drive photography. What matters is that the construct can be sufficiently differentiated to be useful and trainable. The brain will happily combine the output of all the constructs it needs for a given task and resolve any degree of overlap and indeed conflict between them.

We know that a well-trained intuition can handle about ten separate judgement constructs at once. To put it another way: your brain can cope with ten channels of thought simultaneously and, in a few microseconds, combine them into a single judgement. Whereas your rational mind follows a step-by-step process – identifying the problem, retrieving the relevant memories, theories and problem solving routines – the intuitive mind can operate on the appropriate ten channels of thought and solve the complexity of judging a potential or actual image in a moment.

But here is the catch: if one or more of those ten channels of thought are not well programmed, or your intuition doesn't know which is the correct channel or channels to use, then it will make a judgement that is biased or employ a shorthand rule called a 'heuristic'. This is the stuff of 'pre-judgement' or, to use the more pejorative term 'prejudice'.

> Think of a construct as a self-contained 'bundle' of skills, ideas and knowledge around a particular issue. When buying or renting a house the word 'location' describes a construct, when driving a car the vehicle's 'performance' is a construct. We understand these constructs – we don't have to unpack them whenever we want to use them.

Cynthia is always willing to act as a judge at international photographic competitions. She was invited to judge an 'open' competition of about 2,000 images and, like her two fellow judges, she was required to score each image from 2 to 5 on a handheld device which consolidated the three scores on a central PC. On average she had 5 to 7 seconds to judge each image.

About a dozen images into the first batch of 200 the first dog appeared. It scored highly. Very shortly after, another appeared, and over the first 200 images three or four images of dogs, of varying quality, came up for evaluation. However, as the judging progressed into the next and further rounds Cynthia became more and more exasperated when an image of a dog appeared and her 4s and 5s became 2s and 3s. 'Oh no', she exclaimed, 'not more dogs!'. The few seconds allowed for the judgement of each image meant that she, along with the other judges, was forced to rely on her intuitive System 1 thinking. However, she revealed, through her marking and her comments, that key channels were not properly constructed and so her intuition was bringing into play a heuristic which said that images of domestic dogs were not appropriate for an international competition. For a wildlife or nature competition she would have been right to rule out an image of a domestic animal as not within the rules – but not within an open competition.

So what was going on here? For anyone who has sat in on photographic judging sessions tales such as this are all too familiar. The reason is that, able though the judges may have been, their intuition – or if you prefer their non-conscious thinking processes – were only partly driven by true expertise across the range of skills and attributes that make a great photographer or, indeed, a great judge of photography. Their thinking looked like Exhibit 3.1.

Exhibit 3.1
Lacking expertise across the range leads to prejudgement

The judges had some well-skilled, deeply embedded constructs driving their non-conscious intuitive judgement. But the big black devil smileys were the prejudices their non-conscious brains were activating because they couldn't find anything more appropriate to help with the problem they were dealing with. Just imagine if the fire chief encountered in the last chapter had stepped back and said: 'In you go men, you need to make a quick job of this, there is probably a lot of valuable kitchen equipment in here.'

So what are the constructs that photographers should focus upon when making that crucial shutter-clicking judgement? The major national and international photographic bodies are in broad agreement that the ten constructs illustrated in Exhibit 3.2 capture the bundle of abilities and skills that you need to master or demonstrate.

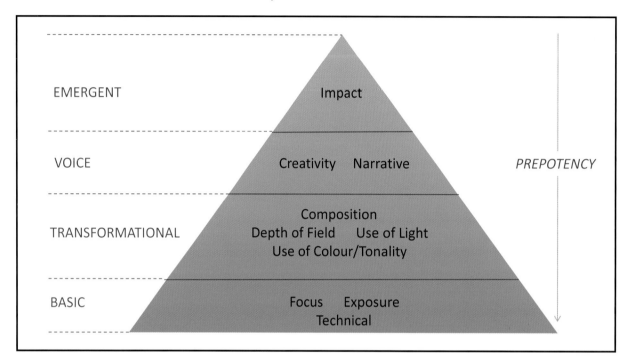

Exhibit 3.2
The hierarchy of constructs

Exhibit 3.2 shows the ten constructs occupying four levels: basic, transformational, voice and emergent. But why put them into levels – surely the top construct, 'impact', is the most important? Shouldn't we be starting with that?

The answer from research into how high-level expertise is created is a resounding no! When we were young we learnt our letters – this process of recognition took time but a certain level of expertise was necessary before we could start the process of recognizing words. From words we move to sentences and all the problems of mastering grammar. From grammar we moved up the process of reading and writing until we reached the level of expertise that has enabled me to write this book. So developing the constructs necessary to be a great intuitive photographer – or, indeed, great at anything else, whether it be sheep farming or astrophysics – is a painstaking and cumulative business.

There are three 'basic' abilities you need to master such that they are completely second nature to you. They are: focus, exposure and technical. These skills are of a higher order of 'pre-potency' than those above them in the hierarchy in that if an image is seen to fail on any of these then the whole edifice of image making collapses. So, if on review, your images are incorrectly exposed or out of crucial focus then you have to revert to that skill and correct the problems before you can move on to the higher-order skills that determine the ultimate quality of the images you produce.

There then follow four 'transformational' abilities: composition, use of light, depth of field and use of colour or tonality in monochrome work. We call these transformational skills because excellence in any of these areas has the ability to 'transform' an image. Use of light, for example, can add drama to an image or it can add an air of mystery or foreboding. It cannot mask poor exposure, inappropriately focused imagery or weak technical skill.

Exhibit 3.3
Wood fires in Orgiva, Spain
– Bob Ryan, 2015
In this image I was struck by the way the morning light shone through and dramatized the smoke from the wood burning in Orgiva, southern Spain. The light both defines and draws our attention – our eyes sweep from left to right absorbing the scene and the mystery imparted by the smoke

Next we have our two abilities that help define our photographic voice or intent. They are both 'primed' by the skills that underpin them but 'telling a story' or 'being creative' are ways of thinking and communicating about what we see. The basic and transformational constructs are the 'language' of photography but they are not its communication. So these two are: creativity and narrative.

The construct of creativity or expression is all about seeing the world anew, of using the photographic medium in new and unanticipated ways to communicate your photographic intent. Unfortunately, creativity has become synonymous with the process of pasting up composite images in ways much favoured in art colleges. Such images can be very creative, tell a story and have impact; however, they do not define what creative means – it has a much broader meaning, as you will see in Chapter 7.

We will also explore the power of narrative in image making. There are some who argue that it is impossible for photography, as a static medium, to ever tell a story. Not so, as I will explain in Chapter 7 – an image has a past and a future, both of which can be reflected in the moment of capture.

But there is one construct left – the ability to create an image that burns into the soul, never to be forgotten. Some images deliver a powerful emotional intensity to the overwhelming majority of people who look at them. This is impact – the ultimate skill in photography. Given any situation we confront

Exhibit 3.4
Iceberg between Paulet Island and the South Shetland Islands, Antarctica, 2005
– Sebastiao Salgado, Genesis Project (Courtesy of NBPictures LLP)
This image had an immense impact upon me when I first saw it hanging in the Natural History Museum, London. It captured, for me, the magnificence of the Antarctic continent and also its fragility

as photographers, there are likely to be multiple ways of telling the story, and many creative interpretations of the subject. But 'impact' is the skill of discriminating between the arrays of choices we face and acting on that which tells the story in the most creative way possible and with highest emotional intensity.

Impact is achieved in two ways: first, it emerges as a product of consummate skill in all the subordinate constructs that make up the great photographer, and, second, it arises through the ability to make choices in the moment of image capture that maximize the emotional intensity the image can deliver. It is this area of photography that the System 2 approach – the rational, pre-visualized image making – cannot capture. It is the Holy Grail of our photographic journey.

> *I was not keen on monochrome photography – it was a genre I had never explored, at least not since my childhood years when my Uncle Fred gave me my first Box Brownie and a roll of 120 film. I was persuaded by a couple of his pals to go to an exhibition of the work of Sebastiao Salgado at the Natural History Museum in London. It was a beautiful day – too good, I thought, for an exhibition in a hot, crowded museum. Still, I paid my entry fee and walked the few steps from the ticket counter into the darkened exhibition hall where over 200 prints from Salgado's 'Genesis' project were hung on light boxes. As I walked in I was confronted by a huge print that stopped me in my tracks. The hairs on the back of my head shot up. The heat and bustle of the city and the museum ceased to exist – in that moment Salgado's image, taken in the Antarctic, delivered its impact. My mind did not need to think about the image, I did not need to analyse it. In an instant I was in the frozen continent, I saw its majesty and its fragility – I also realized what monochrome photography was all about.*

You might at this point have a bit of a mental rebellion: 'I know all about focusing, exposure, composition, depth of field, etc. What can they teach me about that? Well, to be truthful, if you know a reasonable amount about photography the answer is not much. But that's not the point.

Our point is that you know it but can your intuition use it? The answer is probably not – well not unless you have been practising photography for a long, long time. It takes a huge amount of unstructured practice to develop the high level of intuitive expertise you need to produce the breathtaking images you dream of. The aim of this book is to help you 'hardwire' the expertise you need into your head, so that you will be able to achieve true mastery in a fraction of the time taken through conventional learning methods. It is how you can hardwire that expertise that we turn our attention to in the next chapter.

4

FIRST STEPS: WHERE ARE YOU NOW ON YOUR PHOTOGRAPHIC JOURNEY?

The first three chapters of this book should have given you a good idea of what our approach to developing expert photographic skills is all about. From this point forward it will be hard, practical advice all the way as we help you explore where you are on your photographic journey.

In this short chapter we will ask you to go on a process of discovery. We want you to discover how your intuitive judgement of an image compares with the working of your logical photographic brain. Our aim is to get your gut and brain synchronized; then, we will show you ways, using the EPF method, to let your intuitive judgement take over the photographic job of taking and reviewing images. In so doing your intuition will take you to levels of photography your conscious brain can never reach.

So, let's take some time out to find out where you are now on your photographic journey. It's time to get some understanding of where you are on the road to becoming a master photographer. To help prime yourself for what lies ahead, we urge you to work through the following three exercises, keeping the results of each for later reference. These are the starting point of your journey.

Priming Exercise 4.1 – aligning the heart and the brain

If you do the following exercise conscientiously, in the way we describe, it will reveal to you those areas where your judgement is in good shape and those areas where you need to focus the most attention.

1. Choose 12 images taken within the last six months. You may have done some simple processing on them but what you should do, after a quick search, is dump your selected images into a new folder or, if you use Lightroom, a new collection. If a friend is willing to help, get them to select 12 images for you from your collection.

2. Using the 12×10 grid in the appendix, or making one yourself, number or name the 12 images down the left-hand side.

3. Do not look at the images before carefully reading these ten judgements you will need to make:

YOUR TEN JUDGEMENTS:

1. Is the focus appropriate for the image? If that means there is a critical point of focus, where is it? Should it be critically sharp but not over-sharpened? Perhaps using artistic blur is more appropriate? Ask: have I captured sufficient strength of focus to bring out and communicate the story?

2. Is the image correctly exposed, with a good histogram well distributed across the range and with no burnout in the whites, and no blocking of the shadows?

3. Are there any technical faults with the image: horizons not level, verticals not perpendicular, poorly controlled noise, distractors pulling the eye away from the area of interest and so on?

4. Is the depth of field correct in realizing my photographic intention or voice? Is the detail appropriate from front to back – have I achieved what I intended? Have I controlled the depth of field correctly to draw the eye to the principal point of interest?

5. Have I used light to its best advantage in realizing my photographic intention? Does the use of light strengthen or weaken the mood of the image I am trying to convey?

6. Is the image composed to best advantage? Is the main subject dominant in the frame? Have I cropped the image to reflect the best composition available in the raw file? Have I made good use of active and empty space? Do I have strength in line, shape and texture in the image? Have I simplified and positioned the elements within the image to best advantage?

7. Have I used colour to maximum dramatic advantage? If working in monochrome, is the tonality of the image well balanced with powerful blacks and strong whites?

8. Does the image tell a story? Can I summarize its story in a few words? How powerful and engaging is the story being told?

9. Have I found a novel way of realizing the image, either technically or through the use of creative perspective or composition?

10. Does the image have emotional impact? Does it excite me or depress me? Does it arouse in me feelings of elation, guilt or pain? How strong is my feeling?

4. Put on some lively, engaging music. Now, bring up the first image for just three seconds. At the end of three seconds blank your display. It is important that the image is not in front of you when you do the next step.

5. As quickly as you can, score the image you have just seen under each construct on a scale of 0 to 10: 0 for awful, 10 for superb, or however you like to name the end points of your scale. If you cannot remember your impression under a given heading, leave a blank. Try not to put something down just for the sake of it – it will impair the significance of your score.

6. Repeat for each of the remaining images, being very careful to give just three seconds to each.

7. What you will end up with, if you put a score in every cell, is a table that looks like this:

Exhibit 4.1

Priming Exercise 4.1 – specimen output

	Focus	Exposure	Technical	Depth of Field	Use of Light	Composition	Colour /Tone	Creativity	Narrative	Impact
1	7	7	7	8	8	3	6	6	7	5
2	6	4	7	8	8	4	6	6	5	6
3	7	7	6	4	7	4	5	2	3	2
4	7	7	7	7	7	2	5	3	4	3
5	5	4	6	8	4	1	4	2	6	2
6	6	5	7	7	2	8	7	2	5	2
7	9	8	8	6	7	8	3	3	5	5
8	8	7	7	6	7	6	6	4	4	5
9	3	5	4	5	7	7	5	3	5	3
10	7	6	7	5	7	4	6	4	5	4
11	7	7	7	4	5	5	3	5	6	2
12	7	7	8	3	7	4	3	5	1	1
AVERAGE	6.6	6.3	6.7	5.5	6	4.9	4.7	3.3	4.4	2.9

Not counting the first two images, average your score under each construct. We jettison the first two in calculating the average, as these were there just to get you going. Now look at the scores and the averages. These tell you what your intuitive judgement says about each image.

8. You will now need a fresh analysis sheet. Put your analysis to one side and read the ten constructs again, keeping the list open in front of you for reference. Score each image again. Do not try to remember what you put down on your previous analysis – that's right: go through them

again and, taking your time and thinking hard, score them afresh (for this you need only do images 2–12).

9. Now, compare your averages: in the first instance it was your intuition driving your judgement; in the second, your logical, rational brain was doing the work.

What you may find is that some of your averages are well aligned, indicating that your intuitive judgement is working well at that level. It doesn't mean that the quality of your judgement is yet of a high order – that's a different thing. Nor does it mean that your judgements of the ten elements are well balanced. You may be giving too much emphasis to one construct over another, like Sian and Adam in Chapter 2. You may not be activating all the constructs when you take an image or when you review it in post-processing and, like Cynthia, you may be bringing something quite irrelevant into your judgement process. You may find that you are only able to score against a few of the constructs when under the three-second regime. Don't worry, this book will help you fix that.

Priming Exercise 4.2 – working with the constructs

Following the EPF method, you will find that your depth of understanding of each of the constructs will deepen. However, there is a fallacy that we must lay to rest. Taking photographs is not the only way to enhance your skill as a photographer. In many circumstances it is the best way, but you can also enhance the power of your photographic judgement every time you look at an image. What follows is a brilliant exercise. It is very powerful and, if you repeat it regularly, it will rapidly become second nature to you. Also, if you ever want to help anyone else with his or her photography, this is the way you should approach your image review.

1. How about some enlivening music to help you along?

2. Find one of your best recent shots and print it out at A4 size on an A3 sheet of inexpensive matte proofing paper. Don't worry about the quality of the print, because you should have it up on your monitor as well.

3. Write ten judgement constructs around the white border of the print: Focus, Exposure, Technical, Depth of field, Use of light, Composition, Use of colour/tonality, Creativity, Narrative, Impact.

4. Carefully review the image you have chosen, making notes around the margin. You may remember that in Chapter 1 I wrote about using System 2 thinking, that is, your rational, analytical brain, to help boost your intuitive power through a process of intellectual 'ju-jitsu'.

Here we are starting to apply that idea.

I selected an image from a recent trip to Slimbridge – the wonderful wetland centre founded by Sir Peter Scott. I caught this bit of moorhen action with my Nikon D810 and 70–200mm f2.8 lens. I was pleased because a 100% chimp had shown immediately that the basics were all good, the shot was top lit but on first inspection I could see that the composition would work well. The colours were strong and although I had used matrix metering I thought that the blacks of the birds' plumage would render well. I suspected I might be a little tight on the action but I felt the shot had energy and a strong behavioural narrative. My intuition told me I had a good shot that could be strengthened in post-processing – I knew it wasn't a prize winner but I wondered why my initial response was rather muted.

Once home I processed the image carefully and this was the image I pulled out of my collection for subsequent and more detailed review. With Meat Loaf's 'Bat Out of Hell' playing, I set to work reviewing the image construct by construct. First I made an A4-size picture on A3 proofing paper, noting comments around the margins as I went through the constructs one at a time.

Impact:
a good vigorous shot that captures attention. However, muted lighting and exposure detracts.

Narrative:
tells the story of cock moorhens engaging in aggressive behaviour.

Focus:
good on eyes, heads and claws.

Creativity:
ok, but not distinctive. Water level shot better.

Exposure:
slightly under exposed with some blocking.

Use of colour:
vivid blue works well with red of beaks.

Technical:
crop too tight? Clarity of birds needs strengthening.

Depth of field:
patterns in water too dominant.

Use of light:
good, not too intense but top light flattens image. Good catch light.

Composition:
central as action is the theme. Inverted triangle strong.

Exhibit 4.2
Priming Exercise 4.2 – critical review of an image

> *As I thought about the image I recognized the importance of the technical issues. A small increase in overall exposure would help lift the image, with some selective clarity adjustment to the birds to help bring them forward from their background. There was nothing I could do about the crop, but the weak point was the creativity in the image. Wildlife photography never gives a second chance but a more creative positioning, perhaps at water level, would have revealed the action at moorhen level rather than human level.*

My intuitive judgement was that I hadn't quite got an image that lifted it above that of a very good record shot. It wasn't what is disparagingly called a photograph of a 'bird on a stick' – it was just a record of behaviour viewed from a human perspective. To get a shot like this requires a high degree of technical skill as the action, when it happens, happens very quickly.

The intuition in the field comes in recognizing when such a shot is possible. Getting the story in a creative and expressive way, with high impact, means you have to react in a second. I was emotionally engaged in the excitement of the action, I was engaged in deep practice where there was a significant risk, at a number of levels, that my image making would let me down. And I chimped immediately, processed the image as soon as I got home and then thoroughly reviewed the image construct by construct. I used the technology and my own work practice to get the feedback I needed. So, whenever you get home from a shoot or see an image that catches your eye, take some time out, put on some music you enjoy and go through the image point by point. Initially it will be a slow job, but very soon it will become second nature and then, as you persevere, it will become automatic.

Priming Exercise 4.3 – the IMP test

The third of our exercises is the Intuitive Mastery of Photography or IMP test. This is a much more intensive test of your intuitive photographic abilities and it will guide you to where you should focus your immediate efforts to improve. To do this review, go to www.bourchierbooks.com and you will be presented with a downloadable scorecard and a file of 20 images drawn from a variety of genres and of varying quality. You can download the images to a folder or you can assess them online. You will be asked to score each image after reviewing it for just three seconds. We will then give you the opportunity to score each image again, taking as long as you like, and using the ten judgement constructs. Downloadable instructions are available on the website.

Once you have completed your assessment your results can be analysed, telling you:

1. Those attributes of an image that most influence your judgement of its quality.

2. Your progress towards intuitive mastery. Using the test helps you form a judgement about those constructs where you need to focus your attention.

3. How well your intuitive appreciation of an image coincides with your analytical evaluation using each of the ten constructs.

Jean was an excellent photojournalist who took the IMP test. She had been a member of the Clikit and Snapit Camera Club for many years, and she did a lot of judging and gave talks around the local club circuit. Intrigued by this approach, she sought my help. She did this exercise exactly as described. I assessed her intuitive judgement of her images and her more detailed IMP analysis. She was a severe judge of her own work and she had confided in me that her photography still disappointed her. She was in a rut. The analysis revealed that her intuition was giving her a ranking reasonably close to that obtained using her IMP results (in formal terms she was about 70% consistent, where 100% is perfect agreement and 0% is, as you might guess, no consistency at all). That was a positive result, but – and this was what she found surprising – her intuition was working off just four constructs: exposure, technical, use of light and – to a minor degree – composition.

What was happening here was Jean had conditioned herself to look for one or two things in an image: 'are there any burnt highlights or blocked shadows?' and 'is it well cropped?'. These are simple rules, like the triage procedures given to non-specialist medics when sorting out who should have priority of treatment when large numbers of people are injured or sick. She was stuck where the non-specialist medics might be, but she wanted to be the equivalent of a leading trauma surgeon on the front line. Her simple triage rules worked reasonably well but they were not helping her improve, especially in developing the higher-order abilities which set the best photographers apart.

If you have worked through the exercises in this chapter, you should have a much clearer idea of where you are on the path to becoming a great photographer.

However, no matter how skilled you believe you may be, we would urge you to build intensive practice regimes under each of the skill sets represented by the ten constructs. Like a cracked record, we repeat the point that you need to build your non-conscious ability to the point that no matter what your photographic intent, your mind is making the key photographic judgements intuitively, reliably and instantly. By doing this you can free yourself of the constraints of the technical and focus on how to express yourself in the best way possible. It is towards this end that we now turn our attention in the next five chapters.

Exhibit 4.3
Mute swan, Slimbridge
– Bob Ryan, 2012
This gorgeous image, displaying the spring plumage of a mute swan, is lifted above the ordinary 'record' shot

5

STRATEGIES FOR DEVELOPING THE BASIC COMPETENCIES

In this chapter we take a fresh look at the basic constructs: focus, exposure and technical. Our job is not to teach you what you know in the way that you know, but to show you how to embed the skills and knowledge under these three headings in the non-conscious workings of your brain. That way, they will be instantly accessible to you as the need arises.

In this chapter we will focus on the abilities that underpin the rest of your photography. They are:

1. Evaluating the focus requirements of a given image – where is the best point to capture full focus in order to achieve the desired outcome?

2. Exploiting the full dynamic range of your camera with a well-distributed exposure, avoiding burnout at one end or blocking at the other and, crucially, making sure that none of the colours are out of range.

3. Ensuring that critical problems like 'noise', 'distractors', camera 'shake' are all dealt with – these are the technical issues.

With these and all the other skills described in the last chapter, it is important to build the emotional connection with the one you are targeting at any point in time. I then demonstrate, through a process of structured exercises and personal vignettes, how to develop the chosen skill through deep practice. The practice is designed to set up photographic situations that are hard and at which you will initially fail more often than you succeed. The third step is to gain the necessary feedback on your performance, and here I demonstrate how to critically appraise your performance under each skill.

Your reference collection

The first step: take your camera to something you enjoy shooting. It may be a steam fair, a wildlife sanctuary or an old cotton mill. It doesn't matter. Take as many shots as you like but when you get home, put your best ten in a collection, processing them to a good standard of sharpness, exposure and technical presentation. Make a note in your diary to look at this 'reference collection' in six months' time. Do not look at them again until that time.

MAKING THE FOCUS JUDGEMENT

Learning to focus the camera is the first skill you learn when you take it out of the box for the first time. But now let us look at the judgments you have to make and then, using the EPF method, you can start the process of embedding the skills and knowledge of focusing accurately under any given situation into your non-conscious mind.

Making the focus judgement comes at two stages: first, at the point you take the image and second, when reviewing the downloaded image. Getting the focus right is something that must be achieved in camera – an out of focus image cannot be corrected in post processing. For the photographer it is the most pre-potent of all photographic skills in that if an image is incorrectly focused, then all of the higher-order judgements and skills are undermined. Photographic judges, professional image editors and photographic examiners will discard or discount any images that are not correctly focused.

Exhibit 5.1
Llyn Dinas, Snowdonia
– Andy Beel, 2015
Here Andy demonstrates his skill at focusing dark against light using contrast to give the image a wonderfully ethereal quality

So you must be able to make, without conscious thought, the key focus judgements. For now, we will assume that you want to achieve critically sharp focus such that either the whole of the image or some element of it, of your choosing, appears perfectly sharp to a viewer standing at a reasonable viewing distance. Later in this section we will look at the inverse of the focus problem – where it is your intention to use blur to creative effect.

You are standing in the corner of a field looking across a meadow towards a beautiful backlit group of trees. Scattered sheep have trees behind them and to the sides but they are dwarfed by the trees. Between you and the sheep are several acres of arable land and – yes – there is a small clear stream in the middle distance. You focus and take the shot. You 'chimp' the back of the camera, bring the image up to 100% at the point of focus and it isn't sharp. What has gone wrong?

TOP TIP: Take control of the focusing. Use a single fixed autofocus point: lock the focus on the point of critical sharpness with the autofocus lock (AF-L) button on the back of the camera. Then, before pressing the shutter, view the shot at 100% magnification in the viewfinder if your camera has that facility.

You are on a wildlife safari; there is a cheetah lying on the ground about 10 metres from your vehicle. You have a long lens on the front of your camera. It is set to f5.6, the light is good and the animal is burying its head in the carcass of a small Thomson's Gazelle it has brought down. You rest your camera on your beanbag and you take the shot. You chimp the back of the camera and the eyes of the cheetah are not sharp – indeed, they are way out of focus. You had it right! But it went wrong?

TOP TIP: Learn to intuitively lock focus with a single AF point and recompose the picture before pressing the shutter release.

What is sharp depends on the image and your intention, but lack of critical focus, where it is required within an image, is very distracting to the viewer. It is also a problem that must be solved in camera – it is not the role of sharpening tools in post-processing to repair an out-of-focus image. When you look at any image, the eye will always be drawn to the area that is most visually clear – in photographic terms, where it is at its sharpest. Focus is a means of directing your viewer's attention to a defined area within the image. These are the things to be thought of in the focus judgement:

What part of the image needs to be critically sharp?

Normally this will be the principal or dominant point of interest. Usually, images have a single principal point of interest, but not always. A walk around an art gallery showing the works of the great masters will reveal that they have multiple points of interest, carefully graded by technique into the one the artist wants you to look at first, second and so on. With a camera, it is not so easy to create multiple zones of varying clarity of focus. So think: where do I want my viewer's eye to go first? With animals and humans, the rule is simple – go for the closest eye. With architectural and landscape shots, you may need to ensure that all, or the majority, of your image space is sharp. With crowds and sports, always look for the point of the action.

Look at the contrast in the background and fine obstructions in the foreground.

On modern cameras autofocus is usually very accurate, but it can be fooled. Poor contrast and poor light can prevent the camera focusing, and even if it does, the results may be disappointing. In low contrast it may help to deliberately push your camera out of focus and then refocus automatically. If all else fails you may decide to go to manual and, if you have it, use live view mode with 100% magnification. When focusing look for potential obstructions – fine grass or branches close to you may not show up through the viewfinder but the camera will surely find them. Wild animals love to hide – there is always something in the way, and even though a half-hidden tiger may make a marvellous shot, it will not look so good if the evil genie operating your autofocus has decided to pick out and focus on a blade of grass several metres in front of the animal's face.

Do you need continuous autofocus options available all the time?

The answer is no, but with the more sophisticated cameras it is possible to track the focus of a moving object using continuous autofocus and even with 3D tracking. In many situations it is unnecessary: still life, architecture and studio work being examples. However, when photographing people in movement, animals, birds or sporting events, focus tracking is a great advantage.

Do you need a tripod or some other support?

There are two reasons why an image might be out of critical focus: firstly, the focus might not be properly set in the camera. A common problem is not releasing and recapturing focus when reframing a shot. Secondly, you may have induced camera shake. It is always best for the master photographer to shoot while handholding the camera. Why? Because you and your camera need to become one and in the moment. Andy has said many times, tongue in cheek, that he sees a tripod as an instrument of the devil – by the time you have set it up, the subject or the light is gone, or you lose the will to live by carrying it around.

Johnson, an ex-army officer, was a crack shot with a rifle. He was employed from time to time, by a national forestry agency, for the job of culling deer. He never failed to drop the animal instantly. He was very clear about the basic requirements for accurate shooting: the first requirement is achieving physical balance with your rifle; the second is becoming so integrated with your rifle that it becomes an extension of your mind. The process of gaining balance is one of being comfortable, with your body well stabilized and your breathing slow and regular. In the cycle of breathing, the point of the outbreath is when your body is at its most still. To achieve harmony with your gun, he said, you need to work with it, personalize it, enjoy it, look after it. You need to have a love affair with your rifle such that the mere lifting of the rifle to your eye is a source of great pleasure.

So it is with your camera. It has to become an extension of your mind such that it no longer forms a barrier between you and the image.

Hours are wasted on landscape shoots as the photographer fiddles with the legs of the tripod and the level of the camera. The process is so protracted that the golden hour of dawn has turned into dusk before they have got it right. And with modern cameras it is rarely necessary unless you are photographing the interior of a building in weak light.

Handholding becomes more difficult the longer the focal length of the lens, but before getting out the tripod consider increasing your shutter speed by opening your aperture or increasing ISO. Consider using a beanbag if in a vehicle, or indeed anything solid, on which to rest your camera. Carry a tea towel in your camera bag and, folding it along its length several times, wrap it around your lens at the point where you hold it. That will have a steadying effect on your camera and will give you that small margin of safety when handholding a tricky shot. But do remember: if you use a tripod or indeed any other means of support you should switch off vibration reduction, particularly if it is in-lens as opposed to in-camera. The support will fool your VR and make the situation worse.

However, it is *not* our job to teach you how to take well-focused shots. What you must be able to do is to make the choice of focus so intuitive that you do not have to think about how to achieve the results you want. That means you need to 'burn in' the problems of focusing. Here are some ideas, applying the EPF principles:

1. **Find a bird sanctuary where you can see flying birds of different shapes and sizes.**

2. **Select appropriate music to suit the joy and drama of flight. The choice is yours but think of music to support your photographic theme.**

3. **Take shots of flying birds, looking to freeze their movement, showing sharp eyes and clear plumage.**

4. **Take shots of birds with just sufficient blur to suggest movement but with the birds' heads crisp and critically sharp.**

5. **Take shots of birds at twilight or early in the morning.**

6. **After each shot, check for focusing accuracy given your intentions. If you fail to realize the sharpness you want, ask why.**

7. **Take all successful shots and review them on your PC as soon as possible. When you go again, focus on the situations where you failed the previous time.**

Try the above with a 70–200 lens focusing on bees around blossoms. Next, try doing the same in poor light or on a misty morning where the contrasts are weak and focusing is more difficult. Handhold throughout. Repeat the process of checking your success and identifying the failures and concentrating on the reasons they have occurred.

In the shot of the Greylag geese in Exhibit 5.2, I deliberately practised focusing and shooting in the half-light of dusk. To get the image I wanted, I needed to shoot at f2.8 to control the depth of field – an important topic I return to in the next chapter – but I also needed to work with the limited light available. The wide aperture made the job of focusing more difficult, as did the low light levels, but technically the shot did everything I wanted in terms of focus. I could only achieve a shot like this in fading light by spending many happy hours, over the years, practising shots like this.

In the pursuit of creative excellence, the master photographer also needs the ability to lose focus effectively and, using the camera like an artist's brush, produce a blurred image showing movement and just enough information to create the narrative and impact they want.

The technique for doing this is straightforward: switch your focus to manual and adjust so that the image is just in focus. Then, if capturing movement, with the shutter speed at 1/30th or less, sweep through your focal point in the direction of movement you want whilst pressing the shutter. If you leave the camera on autofocus you risk the creation of a

Exhibit 5.2
Greylag geese in flight
– Bob Ryan, 2014
This shot was taken under the most difficult lighting conditions. The image works at many different levels but the key skill exercised here is one of focusing on the fast-moving birds against a background that minimizes the contrast available for the camera's focusing system

Exhibit 5.3
Southern Alaskan
Brown Bear, Katmai
Peninsula

– Alison Price, 2008

In this close encounter with a brown bear Alison wanted to capture the violent shake of the head as the bear resurfaced after having failed to catch a fish. By pinpoint focus on the nearest eye and a slow shutter speed she was able to capture the movement but retain critical sharpness where it mattered

'hard edge' in the image that is horribly distracting and can ruin the shot. It is easiest when using a long lens in excess of 100mm and you may need to close the aperture and pull down the ISO to the lowest native position your camera will accept. If all else fails, a neutral density filter may be needed to slow your shutter speed – remember also that the faster the movement, the easier it is to blur the action.

So, to practise using the EPF principles: find some appropriate music, practise with the hardest subject you can find and immediately chimp and check, reshooting until you get the effect you want. Do you love forests? Go and do some blurry shots of trees, or if the season is right – shoot the bluebells. If you love animals or the kids, why not use them as a subject?

TOP TIP: Build a journal of your photographic journey. Buy some photographic proofing paper and print your images (A4 size is sufficient), leaving a useable margin around the edge. Note the date, time and location, shooting details and any processing notes around the edge. Note also why the image works or why it doesn't. It is important to also jot down how you felt and anything significant about the circumstances when you took the image that would remind you how you felt at a later point in time. We discuss the use of such cues and how they can be created in Chapter 8 on impact. Pop your rough proofs in a file and keep them in date order. Look at them and think about them regularly.

What is acceptable sharpness?

Acceptable sharpness is a term used to describe the apparent sharpness of the image from the viewer's perspective. It depends on a number of things:

- The output medium – projected image or print and, where print, the type of paper used: gloss, matte, semi-gloss or any one of a number of specialist finished paper.

- The age and capacity of the capture medium or method – we are likely to be more accepting of 'softness' when generated by a Box Brownie or, indeed, a mobile phone or tablet than we are of a modern high-resolution digital camera.

- The proposed viewing distance – if an image is to be viewed (say) within 1 metre, then the standard of acceptable sharpness will be much higher than when being viewed at 10 metres.

- Current accepted standards and personal taste – in certain genres, such as wildlife and macro work with bugs and such, sharpness must be perfect. The range between being soft and, equally bad, over-sharpened is very fine indeed. Picture editors and publicity professionals tend to prefer, depending on the subject matter, simple shots that are sharp throughout from front to back.

- The picture style – as noted above, deliberate blur can focus our attention on movement. Capturing blur effectively is a surprisingly difficult art that deserves deep practice in its own right.

Sharpness is not the be all and end all of photography, as the f/64 Group of eminent San Francisco-based photographers thought. Henri Cartier-Bresson referred to it as a 'bourgeois concept' and showed a happy disregard for accurate focus or sharpness in many of his images. Pictures do not become more real or truthful when they are critically sharp. Some of the best and most memorable pictures ever taken by today's standards are not sharp. So, to repeat the point: sharpness has to be appropriate for the style and use of the picture. The focus judgement is about knowing, non-consciously and automatically, what is right for a given shot.

MAKING THE EXPOSURE JUDGEMENT

Like focus, achieving the exposure you intend is a basic competency that is hard to correct in post processing. The modern camera is capable of handling up to 14 'stops' of light intensity from the bright highlights in an image to the blacks. The human eye can distinguish over 20. What looks bright to you will be registered as a burnt-out patch of light when you download your image. Burnt highlights are more problematic than blocked shadows because a viewer's eye is always drawn to the brightest parts of an image and so it is difficult to hide the problem.

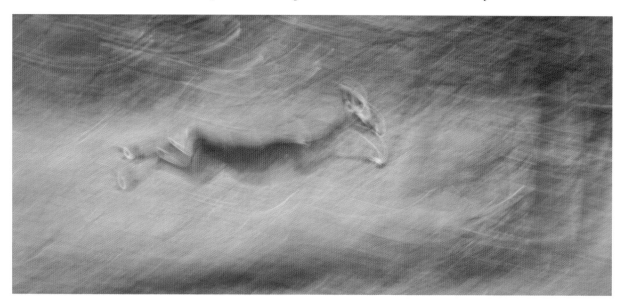

Exhibit 5.4

Impala in flight

–Bob Ryan, 2010

Here I have used a long lens and an out-of-focus technique to capture the movement of an impala in flight. The skill here is to convey movement using the camera like a brush, sweeping through the fleeing animal and mimicking its movement

As you develop your abilities in judging exposure, you will gather a powerful sense of the most appropriate exposure settings to deliver a given mood to your images. Indeed, after regular and sustained practice you will be able to judge the amount of light and the ISO, shutter speed and aperture settings that will deliver the outcome you want.

So, how does the EPF process work here? You need to be able to anticipate, without conscious thought, the potential problem areas within an image and select the most appropriate metering modes for the situation. Where there isn't high intensity in the lighting, you may find that the 'matrix'-metering mode is all that's needed. Where there is, you will need to switch to spot or centre-weighted and expose for the brightest part of the image. Between spot and centre-weighted metering, Andy Beel prefers the latter, as it gives more importance and therefore better exposure to the highlights.

For his style of photography, matrix metering overcompensates for the mid-tones and shadows and can overexpose the highlights. I, on the other hand, confronted with fast-moving action shots, would use matrix metering to overcome the problem, albeit at some cost of having to continuously re-meter.

TOP TIP: All camera manufacturers' metering systems are different, so experiment with metering modes in different situations and see what works best for you.

It is at this point that you may decide to move to manual mode and take over the judgements about both aperture and shutter speed. In manual mode you can meter the scene using your chosen metering mode and then set the shutter speed and the aperture to correctly expose the shot. Once done, you are in a position to reframe and lock focus using your back camera focusing. You now have full control of your camera and can ensure that it is doing what you want rather than what a software engineer on the other side of the planet thinks is best for you. Most nature and wildlife photographers compromise and use aperture priority so that they can control exposure through both aperture and ISO, balancing the two to get the best shutter speed.

However, whatever metering mode you decide to use, you need to achieve the best possible exposure by balancing lights and darks and making sure that the histogram you achieve is balanced and a little to the right. The maxim is: expose for the highlights, process for the darks. It is important to avoid 'blinkies'– a term I give to the warning mode in some cameras that a captured image is out of range either at the top end or at the bottom.

TOP TIP: What you see on the rear monitor is the 'in-camera' processed JPEG version that has a dynamic range one or even two stops less at both ends when compared with what should have been captured in the original raw file. If you are shooting raw, minor blinkies can often be recovered in post-processing. This is a good reason for always shooting raw.

What do you do if the scene has a dynamic range that is just too wide for the camera and there is no time to react? Expose for the highlights and take the shot, then get a filter out of the bag. A polarizer, for example, will lose a stop of exposure; alternatively, a neutral density filter could help solve the problem. If your camera is on a tripod or well supported by a beanbag or similar, then bracket the exposure (some cameras do this automatically).

Exhibit 5.5

Norwich Cathedral cloisters

– *Andy Beel, 2013*

The exposure for this high-contrast shot of the cloisters interior was based on the brightest tones of the exterior to retain detail in the highlights. The exposure compensation was minus 2 stops. This was just sufficient to deliver the strong sense of contrast with strong light and deep shadows that still retain their detail

You will then have the option to blend the images in your post-processing software to achieve the result you want.

The intuitive photographer also has his or her finger hovering near the exposure compensation button. Consider the situation where the frame of your camera is dominated by a subject that is a tone darker than the mid-grey your camera expects. If you expose for the light reflected from that subject, the camera will assume it is reading mid-tone grey. That beautiful black jacket the waiter is wearing will come out a sludgy grey. So you underexpose by knocking two to three stops off using the exposure compensation control and shoot again. What do you have? A wonderful black coat – sadly, the waiter has moved away and you lost the shot. You should have got it right the first time.

At the other end of the spectrum, you are faced with a wedding dress. The opposite is the case. You spot meter off the dress and shoot. The camera shows that beautiful fabric as a rather yucky grey. So this time you adjust your exposure compensation up two to three stops to capture the white. What do you do if the groom in his dark suit is kissing the bride in her white wedding dress? You go for the biggest problem (invariably getting the light object properly exposed) and handle the problems of the dark suit in post-processing.

So, the skill in exposure is not only assessing the dynamic range you must cope with but also the tone of the subject relative to 50 per cent mid-tone grey. So how do you develop this basket of skills? Go out and look for difficult objects to shoot both in high light conditions and in the dark. Churches and the interiors of public buildings on a bright day can be wonderfully challenging – as can busy street scenes at night lit by brightly shining lamps. Indeed, all lights offer the opportunity for some seriously deep practice.

Exhibit 5.6 was taken in a gale, on a cliff top on the north-east coast of Scotland. The aim was to get a perfect representation of the creamy white plumage of the two birds against the gunmetal grey of the sea in the background. I knew that when I looked over the edge the two birds on their nest just a few feet away would look up. I have to admit that my primary emotional state was one of fear as I looked over the edge of a 100 foot drop to the rocks below. I took three shots in all: the first one you see (Exhibit 5.6) was captured as soon as I managed to gain a clear line of sight to their nest, the following two in the few seconds before they turned away.

So, to reinforce the skill of exposure, always try to capture images in difficult light, looking for the best exposure to render the tones in camera.

TOP TIP: Copy the best work of others.[1] **Take any of the photographs in this book and see if you can repeat them or indeed improve on them. If you are lucky enough to be out with a top photographer, ask if you can copy their shot, promising not to use the image for any other purpose than practice.**

---

[1] We do not advocate cheating or plagiarism which is copying the work of others and claiming it as your own. If you are worried about the idea of copying the work of others, why not read Austin Kleon's *Steal like an Artist* (New York: Workman Publishing Company, 2012) and discover the secrets of all great artists who borrowed ideas from each other.

Exhibit 5.6

Gannets over a cliff edge in Scotland

– Bob Ryan, 2015

The intention of this shot was to capture the beauty of the birds against the inky blackness of the sea, several hundred feet below. Working in storm conditions heightened the emotional intensity I felt and, I believe, influenced the response of the two birds to me

So, the strategy for burning-in exposure skill is repeated practice. On a bright day, preferably in the morning or evening, take the camera somewhere the light will be a challenge. It could be your front hall, your street, the local town centre – it doesn't matter. Get some appropriate music playing on your headphones and in manual mode practise shots using both spot- and centre-weighted metering. Check constantly. Practise adjusting your exposure using your exposure compensation button, looking for the perfect histogram for the scene you are trying to capture. Also, if you are using aperture or shutter priority, get used to locking your exposure when you spot-meter. Why? Otherwise, as soon as you reframe or refocus, your camera will alter your measured exposure. If you are in manual mode it isn't needed – spot-meter and set your shutter speed and aperture and you can then happily reframe, refocus and take the shot.

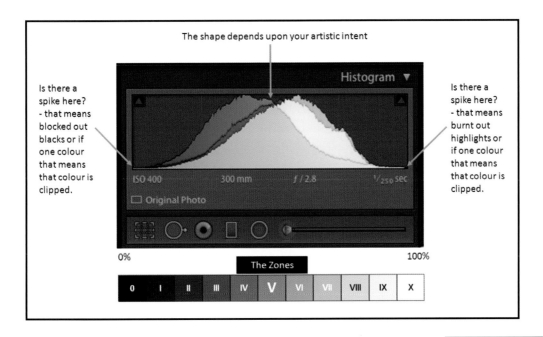

The shape depends upon your artistic intent

Is there a spike here? - that means blocked out blacks or if one colour that means that colour is clipped.

Is there a spike here? - that means burnt out highlights or if one colour that means that colour is clipped.

Histogram ▼

ISO 400   300 mm   f / 2.8   ¹/₂₅₀ sec

Original Photo

0%   100%

The Zones

0 I II III IV V VI VII VIII IX X

Remember, the histogram you see in your camera is a truncated, JPEG version of your image. In Exhibit 5.7 I show, as an example, the more representative histogram you will see in Lightroom. The key thing when taking the shot is to avoid clipping the highlights (burnt out with no recorded detail), and as you take your image from the camera to your processing software you will soon recognize the range of what is possible. The histogram below shows an image that is of average brightness but with good contrast – you may want a high-key image, and in that case the histogram will be bunched to the right. With a low-key (dark) image, it will be bunched to the left.

The width of the histogram measures the image contrast and is more important than the shape. The height of the histogram at any point measures the 'pixel count' or intensity of light falling in each of the tonal ranges. Under the histogram I show the tone zones, ranging from mid-grey at the mid-point through to black at the extreme left and white at the extreme right. The extreme ends of the histogram are called the white point and the black point.

TOP TIP: Try a variable 2–8 stop neutral density filter to give complete control over predetermined ISO, shutter speed and aperture.

Exhibit 5.7

Histogram and tone scale

GETTING THE TECHNICALITIES RIGHT

Go out, near dawn or sunset depending on the light conditions, and get close to a tall building. You may not use a tripod, but you want a pin-sharp, well-exposed, technically excellent shot. You are no longer worried about the focusing and exposure issues: they are well practised. You do want to get the other technical bits right. You need a high ISO to cope with the relatively low light but you want to avoid too much noise in your final image. You need as shallow a depth of field as possible. You also want a good frame-filling shot, with strong backlight, straight and vertical uprights. You want to avoid distractors: your point of interest is the building in front of you, not the rubbish can to the right in the foreground.

So, how do you deal with this? Your artistic intent is a first-class record shot – you may question why you want such an image, but I will take that as your artistic intent. Here is how the intuitive photographer works:

- Select lens or set zoom to (say) 35mm

- Set ISO (possible 640 maybe higher)

- Set manual mode

- Set exposure to brightest part of the scene

- Select point of interest

- Focus using back of camera focus lock

- Reframe and shoot.

To your horror, you realize that the horizon is not level, or your verticals are out of plumb. Your verticals are converging and the rubbish bin is still there. Worse still, you have clipped the top of the building.

What has gone wrong? You forgot to look – that is, really look through the viewfinder. Most people who handhold tend to get the camera out of line with the horizon by a set number of degrees – so practise compensating your hold. If you come in tight on any object, being able to get the geometry right, without thought, is a vital skill. How do you deal with converging verticals? Shoot from a distance that allows you to effectively hold the plane of the camera's sensor vertical. Most people do not make sure they can see the whole of their viewfinder window; they hold their eye away from their camera and as a result what they are seeing and what the camera is seeing are two different things. So glue your eyeball to the viewfinder (please don't take that literally) and scan all round the frame. See as your camera sees — look through it and not into it.

TOP TIP: If you have a camera with an electronic viewfinder, the size of the EVF may be variable so you can see it all even when wearing glasses, and it will also have an electronic level. DSLR users may have access to a live view mode and most have a virtual horizon in either the viewfinder or the live view mode of operation.

TOP TIP: The only way to avoid converging verticals in-camera is to ensure that the vertical plane of the sensor is in the same vertical plane as the building. You can resort to a tilt/shift lens, or simply get further away from the building. Another alternative may be a vertical panorama shot.

We met Alison in Chapter 1. You may remember that Alison started her photographic career, in the pre-digital era, as a scene of crime photographer. She had to work a scene methodically and quickly, making sure every image counted. She learnt that details matter: accurate focus, well-lit images and precise and careful framing. The first requirement of her job was learning to look — consciously sweeping the image through the viewfinder, making sure all the details were in frame. Everything that was unnecessary to the image was excluded. She learnt the skills of positioning — 'the best zoom is your legs' was her favourite phrase. Learn to move your body backwards and forwards and don't be afraid to get down low or stretch up high. 'Work the subject', she said, 'and your camera will work for you'.

TOP TIP: You cannot wear your pixels out — keep shooting until you are sure that you have recorded your intention. Every shot you take is an opportunity to get it right all the way through the picture taking and making process. If you only take one shot, you must be absolutely certain it is what you wanted in a single frame.

As with focus and exposure, we propose the same procedure for driving these three basic photographic constructs into our non-conscious minds so that thinking about them, making the right choices and opening the space for creativity and impact in our photography become entirely automatic. Here are the key points with each:

- Set time aside, as regularly as you can, to engage in the deep practice needed to embed the chosen constructs in your subconscious.

- Do not try to do them all together – it doesn't work. Focus on focus, focus on exposure and focus on the technical aspects of creating a first-class image but do it separately. Do not worry about missing focus if you are practising exposure and vice versa.

- Gear up your brain with some emotionally charging music and make sure you are focused on the job. Forget the washing, the children or the job just for a moment and revel in the joy of deep-learning your photography.

- Look for opportunities that will push your skills in each of these three areas to the limit. If you think your focusing is spot on, try catching a swallow or a house martin in flight – handheld, in poor light.

- As soon as you take the shot – chimp the image. As soon as you get back home, download and review the images, noting carefully what went well and most importantly what went wrong.

- Where things have gone wrong, focus on them. We love to practise the things that are easy, but perfection comes from practising what is hard.

- Keep practising the basic skills no matter how good you are. The more you do the better you get and, although the changes are subtle, as the months roll by your photography will get better and better.

Finally, when you have practised these skills for six months, go out to your favourite location again, take some more images and put them in your reference collection with the ten you reserved at the start of this chapter. Compare them – and be very surprised. Even now your photographic skill has jumped to a new level. You may not be an Art Wolfe or a Joe Cornish yet, but you are on your way! In the next chapter we ramp up your skill set by looking at those photographic constructs that can transform your photography.

TOP TIP: Why not read the previous chapters again? Have a go at marking up those sections that you know you would like to work on some more. Have you done the priming exercises in the previous chapter? If you have a paper copy, get out your pen and make margin notes. Make this book yours.

Exhibit 5.8
Eilean Donan Castle
– Bob Ryan, 2013

This image of one of the most photographed castles in the world captures its grandeur in the light of the setting sun. I elected to portray the castle using critically sharp focus and a well-balanced exposure across the dynamic range. Technically I took care not to over-sharpen the image, made sure the horizon was absolutely level and the crop heightens focus on the castle as the primary object of interest. From the perspective of the basic photographic constructs, the image scores highly. But how well does it stand up at the next level, when we consider the transformational constructs – use of light, colour, composition and depth of field?

6

STRATEGIES FOR DEVELOPING THE TRANSFORMATIONAL ABILITIES

'At a speed of 365,000 miles per second you will never catch
the light – just wait for it to come to you.'

– Bob Ryan

This chapter builds upon the last using the same EPF method – again by looking for photographic subjects under technical constraints that enforce deep practice. For example, with the use of light, we seek situations where there is likely to be very high light contrast that stretches the dynamic range of the camera and your ability to use varying light intensity productively within the image. Again, feedback is crucial, but this time it is through the medium of 'rough proofing' using very restricted post-processing.

Why are these the transformational abilities? The reason is that each one has the power to transform your photography from the ordinary to the extraordinary. But, just like those at the basic level, each one is a collection of different skills, expertise and knowledge.

There are four transformational abilities, each of which calls for a wide range of different types of expertise:

• Depth of field

• Use of light

• Composition

• Use of colour/tonality in black and white.

Each is a means through which you can better express your creative intent. Expertise in judging the appropriate depth of field builds upon the basic skills of focus explored in the last chapter. Use of light builds upon the basic skills of exposure, and composition builds upon the technical. The fourth one represents a new bundle of skills: how to balance colour and tone in an image to greatest effect. When working in monochrome we still need that fine sense of colour and tone as we look for the range and depth of contrast across a scene.

DEPTH OF FIELD

In most images there will be a particular point where you want your viewer to look. It might be the result of his or her visual journey through the image, or it might be a point where you want the impact to be delivered. Depth of field controls the viewer's perception of the relationships between the subject matter and the surrounding background or environment. This technique can be used to strengthen or break those implied connections.

Extended depth of field is extensively used in narrative-type pictures to reinforce real or implied relationships. Look back at Alison's image of the dying infant orang-utan in Chapter 1 or my image of the Greylag geese taking off at Slimbridge in Chapter 5, and you will see how the depth of field has been controlled to hold your attention on the key points of interest in the image. Depth of field, or DoF for short, determines what is in focus and what is not. The human eye automatically goes to the sharpest point in an image and so we can isolate the most important elements from both their background and their foreground by exploiting both aperture and focus.

In Exhibit 6.1, I wanted to focus on the owl's eye. I wanted the viewer to marvel at its clarity and its beauty. The rest of the bird was the obvious context and offered a beautiful frame designed by Mother Nature. The shot was taken in a barn on a wet day, in poor light, at the Newent Raptor Centre in Gloucestershire. I did not want the wooden wall behind the bird's head to distract the viewer, nor did I want any of the other onlookers to impinge on the shot. So, I chose to use a 300mm prime lens at f2.8 shooting at ISO1600. With aperture priority as the shooting mode, I achieved 1/400th of a second under the given light conditions, which was more than enough to freeze the moment when the handler held the bird aloft.

The use of a long lens, in close proximity to the subject and at its widest aperture, has served to blur out all background detail completely. It has also softened the peripheral feathers around the head and down the neck. As you look closely at the image, the background has been smoothed out to a colour that matches the feathers of the bird. The closest plumage is also slightly 'soft'; all that is sharp is the eye, the beak and the intervening feathers.

Now consider the opposite extreme – what I sought in Exhibit 6.2 was a 'picture postcard' shot of the palace in the Generalife Gardens alongside the Alhambra in Granada, Spain. The problem I faced was to create an image, avoiding the people who visit the gardens every year, and for it to be as sharp as possible from front to back. The time of the visit was, unavoidably, when the sun was high. So, to capture the full depth of field I used a 50mm prime set at f16, which with a low ISO of 200 gave a shutter speed of 1/100th of a second – quick enough to guarantee a pin-sharp shot. The small aperture gave a wide depth of field, but to maximize the range of acceptable focus it was necessary to guesstimate the hyperfocal distance.

Exhibit 6.1
Owl, Newent Raptor Centre
– Bob Ryan, 2011
With this image I wanted to focus on the beauty and clarity of the owl's eye. The sharpness and clarity of the eye and beak stand in contrast to the soft plumage and the well-rendered background

TOP TIP: Normally, the focal length of the lens dictates the minimum shutter speed required to achieve a critically sharp shot. So, a 50mm focal length should permit a minimum shutter speed of 1/50th of a second. With deep practice you should be able to handhold at a shutter speed slower than this, especially if your camera or lens has image stabilization.

The hyperfocal distance is the point of focus where the image is sharp from halfway between you and the point of focus and from there through to infinity. There are two ways of determining that point: a hard way and an easy way. The hard way is to get out the tables or an app, dial in the make of camera, the lens, the aperture, what you had for breakfast (not really) and get the measurement in feet or metres. Some lenses have a scale on the barrel that gives a good indication of the distance to the focal point. Once you have done all that, you point and shoot.

Now the easy way – it takes practice – but once mastered you stop thinking about it and finding the correct focal point becomes very intuitive. This is how it's done: in manual mode, spot-meter off the brightest part of the scene. Then, using your thumb on the back focusing button, guesstimate the point one-third of the way into the scene, focus and, with a free finger, check with the 'depth of field' indicator to see if you have it right. If it is, rebalance the composition, holding the focus locked, make sure the horizon is level and take the shot. As you can see, the photographic intention of creating a 'pretty' record shot has been achieved in Exhibit 6.2 in just a few seconds.

Exhibit 6.2
Generalife, Granada, Spain
– Bob Ryan, 2015

This picture postcard shot was taken focusing on the hyperfocal distance in order to achieve an image that was sharp from foreground to background

TOP TIP: Four 'levers' control depth of field:

1. The size of the sensor (the bigger the sensor, the more control you have).

2. The focal length of the lens (longer lenses give less depth of field).

3. The chosen aperture (wider aperture gives less depth of field).

4. The distance to the point of focus (the closer you are to the subject, the shallower will be the depth of field).

The opposite uses of these four levers will deepen the DoF.

Now, to practise: devise a critically challenging situation – one where the potential for failure is real, select any object in the middle distance (at about 50 metres distance) and practise taking shots of varying depth of field. Remembering the EPF procedure and using a zoom lens to start (a 70–200mm lens is ideal), work the shot with varying apertures. Take some shots low and some shots high. Advance towards your chosen object, taking ten steps at a time, and repeat, chimping your images as you go. Remember to use the 100% magnification function if you have it set up, and then at the end of your shoot, get the images downloaded as quickly as you can and choose the best ten with varying depth of field. Print the images on matte proofing paper. Make notes on the margins of your settings to help reinforce your deep learning.

What you will notice, given that you have been proceeding with the deep practice we recommend, is that in comparison to your reference photographs there is a noticeable increase in the quality of your image making. You will almost certainly find that in concentrating on this new level of skill, the lower levels are starting to emerge non-consciously in your shooting. If this is the case, you are well on your way to mastery of your art.

As with all things artistic, there is always an opposite view or technique. Andy has a huge portfolio of prints based on the idea of limited depth of field, where only a small area of the picture is acceptably sharp. The concept is that the viewer will look for and at areas that are sharp and they therefore dominate the composition. This idea can be used on various levels. Initially the point of focus can be placed on the motif or the subject matter of the picture that is intended to provide dominance within the composition. If limited depth of field is used, then the clarity of the foreground and background will be subdued, hence breaking the relationships between the subject matter and its environment.

A more interesting idea is to not focus on the subject matter and to place the area of sharpness in such a way that the viewer's eye needs to move through the picture space to reveal the unsharp subject matter, as in Exhibit 6.3. The 18mm wide-angle lens was focused on the foreground. The subject of the picture is the person on the light-toned path wearing a dark-coloured coat. If he had been wearing a light-coloured coat, the picture opportunity would not have arisen because the contrast of tones between the coat and the path would not have been present.

TOP TIP: What Andy has done in Exhibit 6.3 is an example of rule inversion. If you come across a rule in photography, try breaking it. Try the opposite, but don't be half-hearted: completely flip the sense of the rule on its head. If you do, the result can often work in surprising ways.

USE OF LIGHT

Of all the transformational skills, the use of light is the one that can have the most profound impact upon your image making. Indeed, the word photography comes from the Greek φῶς (*phōs*), which means 'light', and γραφή (*graphé*), which means 'draw'. Literally, photography is 'drawing with light'.

Light can be described using many different words. Here are just a few: hard, soft, dull, transient, low, high, glancing, ethereal, contrasty, rim, side, front, back, dappled, three-quarter, the golden hour, the afterglow, cathedral lighting, God's fingers, dreek (Scottish sunshine), wet, point, diffused, pastel. The list is like a mini-dictionary and for good reason. The quality of different lights imparts different moods and atmosphere to an image.

What matters is to find the appropriate lighting for the subject you have chosen and for your intent to either describe or to interpret the subject. In many cases it's a matter of planning to be in the right place at the right time with the appropriate lighting to communicate your vision and intent. For example, taking street photography after a shower of rain when the sun is shining will produce very high contrast and therefore hard, detail-less

Exhibit 6.3
Royal Avenue, Bath. 18mm f2.0
1/640 200 ISO

– Andy Beel

Here, Andy has used the technique of 'rule inversion' making the middle and foreground sharp. This takes your eye through the image to the out-of-focus subject in the far distance

shadows. If your intent is to produce pastel colours and soft contrast, then you are in the right place but at the wrong time with the wrong lighting.

Capturing the right or appropriate light for a scene is a difficult art that may entail that you use flash to balance harsh natural light in a shot.

Exhibit 6.4
Light burst, Westonbirt
Arboretum

– Bob Ryan, 2015

This image exploits a dramatic use
of light by careful positioning of the
source behind the trunk of the tree

However, the very best light, outside of a studio setting, is the light nature gives you. Light has a powerful effect on mood, so in this section choose your elevating music to best match the moment. Take, for example, Exhibit 6.4, shot at the 'Enchanted Christmas' event at Westonbirt Arboretum. It was a cold, misty night after heavy rain, giving the lights an ethereal quality. Of the many shots taken that night, one caught my eye: a rather nondescript tree with a powerful arc light behind it. The effect was startling.

Generally, light is at its best in the early morning and late evening, for about an hour before and after the sun rises or sets. This is because its shallower angle will produce shadows that add volume and form to a subject or landscape. The exercise that follows is best done on a cloudy but windy day so the cloud is moving and hence the light is changing. Take any simple street scene and practise taking multiple shots using the EPF principles. Take your time watching and shooting the varying light as it breaks or fades depending on the time of day.

Priming Exercise 6.1

Here are the steps to follow:

- Choose your music and make sure you are properly clothed for the time of year. Dawn in the northern latitudes can be very chilly!

- Use a prime lens if you have one – a 50mm is ideal. If using a zoom, set it on 50mm and don't change it.

- Decide upon the subject of your photography – perhaps a church in the distance or a row of houses. You will find that an image with strong contrasts and maybe some interior lights shining out will add to the complexity of the problem.

Exhibit 6.5
Indian safari
–Bob Ryan, 2015
In this early-morning shot, I saw the gorgeous morning light and, handholding my camera in a moving Land Cruiser, took the shot

- Work the scene, taking multiple shots (spot-metering is likely to work best). Vary your technique from silhouette to full tonal range.

- Focus on a point of interest and look for shooting positions where the light enhances that element of the image.

- Remember to keep chimping and, when you get home, download and rough proof your ten best images, making notes to yourself of why they worked.

Exhibit 6.6
Andy, somewhere in southern Spain
– Bob Ryan, 2015
Here, my personal challenge was to use the sun backlighting the tree to enhance the contrast and to add luminosity to the scene

TOP TIP: Whenever you see startling light, take a shot. Master photographers always have a camera with them, even if it is only their mobile. Become a 'light junkie' – develop a light compulsion – take it when you can, hunt it down and do whatever you can to get back to a scene when the light is likely to be at its most effective.

An important element of the use of light judgement is working out the direction the light is coming from and its potential impact upon an image. In Exhibit 6.6, note how the position of the light behind the tree adds vibrancy and impact to the shot. Ask yourself the following questions: does the shot work? Does it have impact? How has the position of the sun as a backlight helped add drama to the shot? Why is it in monochrome?

Priming Exercise 6.2

To help with all this, work through this straightforward tabletop experiment: place a small, irregularly shaped object in the centre of a table in a darkened room. Put your camera on a tripod (yes, I give you permission to use one for this exercise) and attach a camera remote or, if you prefer, use a five-second delayed shooting mode. Now, with some great music in the background and using a small pen torch,

Exhibit 6.7
Eilean Donan Castle
– Bob Ryan, 2016
Do you remember the image of Eilean Donan Castle in Chapter 5? Now look at this reinterpretation showing the drama of a stormy sky and a glancing band of sunlight moving rapidly across the scene. I spotted the gap in the clouds advancing from the south-west and recognized the possibility of capturing this shot

take photographs with its light directed on the object from different directions: front, back, sideways left and right, and overhead. Then as quickly as you can download your shots, look at them with the same music playing and think hard: which one is the most dramatic, which one brings out the texture of the object and which its colour? I do not tell you the answers to this – you must discover them for yourself.

You can repeat this exercise but varying the size and quality of the light. Notice the shape and quality of the shadows that are produced if a small, hard point source of light is used. What happens to the shadows as you move the point source of light very close to and at a distance from the subject? Now repeat using a large, soft light source close to and far away from the subject. What happens to the quality of the shadows now?

Moving away from the tabletop, find an opportunity to repeat the exercise using a familiar object (perhaps an isolated tree in a field) and circle it, taking images when the sun is bright but low in the sky. Repeat with the sun at mid-morning, midday and mid-afternoon. Use a 50mm lens or lower. Practise blocking the low sun using a branch or similar, but be careful. I repeat: be careful with the sun, particularly when using telephoto lenses – scorching your retina is not pleasant, it is very dangerous and can lead to an early termination of your photographic career.

TOP TIP: Be very careful when photographing the sun through the lens viewfinder found on the conventional DSLR. The sun is a gorgeous object in any shot, but use live view mode even if it means swapping to a second camera.

Keep repeating the above exercise wherever and whenever possible until you know, without thinking, where the sun is and its potential impact upon your image. Remember, with this exercise as with all others in this book, that you remember to forget – not to forget in the sense of never having known, but to forget in the sense of not needing to remember what you know. You just know.

TOP TIP: Reflect on these three quotations: John Ruskin, a 19th-century painter and art critic, urged his pupils to 'think in shadows'. John Blakemore, photographer and printer, on the subject of shadows, said 'living dark, dead black'. Finally, shadows are the soul of a black and white photograph.

COMPOSITION

Composition, like the other constructs at this level, is vital to the creation of a great image. Your job is to make composing just like breathing – you do it automatically – a reflexive act as soon as you determine the object you are photographing. The point of composition is to direct your viewer's attention to your chosen point of interest and also to communicate the story in the most effective way. I will focus more on the storytelling element when I discuss narrative at the next level. For the moment I will seek to burn in the skills of placement and the role of line, shape and pattern in building an image.

Composition can be best described as spatial coherence – actual and implied. What that means is that when looking at an image, do its elements fall naturally into place? Poor composition is like bad grammar – when you see it, it jars, it's like a wrong note in a piano sonata. Sometimes misplacement works through its unsettling effect, but usually it distracts the viewer and undermines your intent. The first element of good composition is the frame space, and in photography we are limited to a square or a rectangle; however, within that frame space we may deliberately choose to limit the image perceptually – commonly to a circle or an oval using a vignette or by deliberate framing of the subject.

The placing of elements within the frame is more art than science. However, the Fibonacci spiral has inspired one of the most well-known rules within composition – the rule of thirds. The ideal proportions for any rectangle were discovered by the ancient Greeks and first formalized by Euclid. The ideal – or golden ratio – is 1.6180 to 1. Using squares and rectangles conforming to the golden ratio, it is straightforward (and quite good fun) to create a spiral which comes to an eye at approximately the one-third position.

Fibonacci's spiral, shown in Exhibit 6.8, can be arranged in any one of four ways; this gives

Exhibit 6.8

The Fibonacci spiral

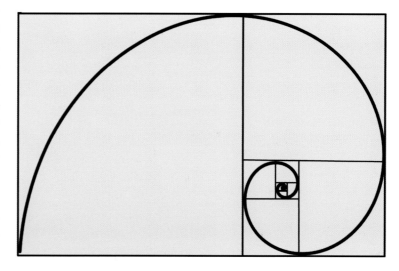

four corner points, and any element positioned at one of those four points falls naturally to the eye. Likewise, elements placed along the spiral itself or, indeed, any of the connecting lines running through the four eyes, also feel more naturally placed.

Exhibit 6.9

The image frame with the principle connections to the eye of the Fibonacci spiral

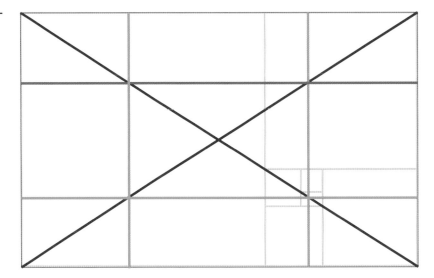

The geometry of this grid should become completely intuitive for you – it doesn't specify exactly where to put all the elements of your image, but it will help you to make spatially coherent choices. If we take Salgado's image of the iceberg in Chapter 3, we can see how he has reflected the rule of thirds, or better the Fibonacci spiral, in the architecture of his image:

Exhibit 6.10

Iceberg between Paulet Island and the South Shetland Islands, Antarctica, 2005

– *Sebastiao Salgado, Genesis Project*
The red lines show how Salgado's image reflects the rule of thirds
(Courtesy of NBPictures LLP)

You will notice that the diagonals in Exhibit 6.9 also pass through the eyes of the Fibonacci spirals, and that elements placed along a diagonal and positioned at those points create a sense of natural tension in an image (see Exhibit 6.10 as an example).

Take any book of images from the great photographers and have a look at their preferred compositional style. Salgado's *Genesis* contains several hundred images, and you will notice how often he uses the 'strong diagonal' from top left to bottom right. Look at other books and see if you can recognize some of the following:

1. The rule of thirds where elements are specifically placed at the corner intersections, the horizontal or vertical lines or, indeed, on the Fibonacci spiral.

2. Triangles leading to a focal point through perspective or in the form of three objects related to one another in a group.

3. The strong diagonal running from top left to bottom right or vice versa (less common).

4. Funnelled perspective through frames at diminishing distances to the eye.

5. Curves leading the eye to a principal point of interest where the curve is continuous or broken and implied.

You will discover that many books have been written on the topic of composition, and Art Wolfe's *The Art of the Photograph – Essential Habits for Stronger Compositions* is one of the best (see the bibliography for further details), but – and it's a big but – the greatest composition tends to work subliminally in the viewer's mind. If someone says of one of your images: 'that's a fine composition', you have probably failed.

Look back at the image of the owl's head at the beginning of this chapter and ask yourself why the image works. We have already worked on the problem of the depth of field and we can note, in passing, the gentle side light that adds quality to the colour and texture of the bird's plumage. But what about the composition – is it quite central? No, the eye is top left. Note also the flow and shading of the plumage. It flows on a downward diagonal from left to right. What you will recognize here is the use of a 'strong diagonal' – the compositional structure isn't thrust down the viewer's throat but it's there all the same, adding a sense of tension and drama to the image. Exhibit 6.11 gives another example.

Exhibit 6.11

Bee-eater, South Africa

– Bob Ryan, 2010

Anticipating the flight of a bird is always difficult, although I recognized that it would fly up and to the left or right of the thorn bush where it was resting. That would give the implicit diagonal I needed to make the shot. In processing I realized I had captured the tiny web which, very close to the edge of perception, reinforces the diagonal and the strength of the composition

Note again the implicit diagonal – at one level the mind recognizes it but at another it doesn't. The diagonal is implied by the direction of the bird's flight, the small thorn bush and the tiny spider's web linking the image to the bottom right corner. With this image the diagonal also connects two story elements in the picture: the bird in flight and where it has come from. This lifts the image away from a simple shot of a bird in flight to one where some of the context, the bird's habitat, is revealed as well.

In classical psychology this phenomenon of making implicit connections within images through careful placement of elements is called 'Gestalt imagery'. There are a number of principles in Gestalt imagery:

1. **Similarity:** when several objects look similar, they will tend to be perceived as a group or a pattern. A number of birds flying together will be perceived as a group.

2. **Anomaly:** where a number of similar objects are perceived as a group, any member of the group can be made to stand out if it has some dissimilarity.

3. **Continuation:** because the eye tends to follow along a line or curve (see Exhibit 6.11), the web and the bush lead the eye directly through to the bird.

4. **Closure:** if a shape is only partially indicated with sufficient points, a viewer will fill in the missing gaps to create the implied shape.

5. **Proximity:** when objects are packed closely together, they appear to form a group.

6. **Figure and Ground:** when a viewer sees a shape, they will differentiate that shape (figure) from its surrounding area (the ground). This is why careful management of depth of field enables the viewer of an image to clearly focus on the subject as the point of interest.

The Gestalt principles give us some important clues about how our viewer will perceive the elements in a given image.[1] As a general rule, one principle point of interest and a maximum of two subordinate points are the most an image can sustain without risking becoming cluttered and overwhelming. The judgement then comes as to the placement of the elements in the frame.

What follows is a sequence of compositional projects using the EPF principles:

• Applying the rule of thirds, create an image where the point of interest dominates the image at the top right intersection.

• Using the same point of interest, include in your composition a 'balancing element' on the other side of the frame.

• If possible, using the same point of interest, look for both overt and implied leading lines.

• See if you can create a balanced composition with your principal point of interest in the centre of your image.

---

[1] For an excellent introduction to the issues of composition and design read Donis A. Donis, *A Primer of Visual Literacy* (Cambridge, MA: The MIT Press, 1974).

- Create an image which has a strong, dominant triangular theme. Create another where the triangle is implied.

- Create an image where your point of interest is framed by something in the foreground (it could be a tree, a building or indeed anything). Work to isolate your point of interest using depth of field, and create another shot such that the frame and the point of interest are sharp.

- Create an image that has clear foreground interest, a middle-ground point of interest and a distant background.

- Create an image with a 'reveal' at your point of interest, just like the figure on the hill in the image at the end of the last section (Exhibit 6.6).

TOP TIP: A great aid to good composition is a small image frame made out of stiff card. Using this, you can focus simply on the job of identifying the compositional potential of a scene without getting into the other issues of photography. The card should ideally be black and stiff enough to take some hard wear. The interior dimension should be 9×6 inches and should give you a reasonable view when held at arm's length.

Good composition is a habit of mind but it is not an end in itself. What matters is what works. So wherever you are, think about what you see in terms of potential images. For example, looking out from your window, you see three chimneys forming an implicit triangle. How could you make a composition of that? It is said that the only rule in composition is that there are no rules. One thing I do urge is not to use 'the rule of thirds' as the default whenever you are stuck thinking of how to compose a shot. Sometimes it is perfect given your photographic intent, but often it can just appear formulaic.

However, by deep practice you will soon learn what works and what doesn't. Here are three great exercises:

Priming Exercise 6.3

1. Take a small camera to a crowded area in town, or where there is a lot of confusing activity under way (your tablet's or mobile's camera will work just fine) and look for images that reflect the

Gestalt principles of Similarity, Anomaly, Continuation, Closure, Proximity, Figure and Ground. Practise placement within the frame to achieve the specific designs you have in mind.

2. Find an image, local to you, that has been published in a good-quality photographic magazine. Look for one that is well composed – one that has sold well or won major competitions is best, but any you judge to be excellent will do. Now go and replicate the image as faithfully as you can. You cannot pass such an image off as your own, but careful copying is, as any sporting coach will tell you, a brilliant way to learn.

3. As you go about your daily business without camera in hand, keep looking for strong compositional shapes and elements: triangles, Fibonacci spirals, leading lines and strong diagonals.

Keep repeating these exercises using the EPF principles and you will soon find your command of composition improves rapidly to the point that it becomes deeply intuitive.

USE OF COLOUR/TONALITY

The popular taste in magazine photography is for strong, saturated colours. It is well recognized in the publishing world that colour is associated with emotion, and picture editors go for those that have a colour 'punch'. However, the expert photographer knows that colour is just one element in the mix required to produce great work. Our task is to understand the ways that colours relate to one another and how the photographer can combine them to create specific effects. Here, our approach is not about the theory of colour – there are some great references on the topic at the end of the book. Our task is to help you develop simple strategies, using the EPF principles, for helping you integrate the use of colour into your photography.

Here is a quick reminder of the basics:

The primary colours are: red, blue and yellow – mixing any combination of colours cannot create these three. The secondary colours are formed from the primaries: red and blue give purple, blue and yellow give green, and yellow and red give orange.

The tertiary colours are any combination of a primary and a secondary to its immediate left or right in the colour wheel (Exhibit 6.12). Because of the way the human eye is built, we perceive white light as a mixture of red, green and blue (RGB) and progressively adding one to another builds the whiteness – thus RGB is referred to as an 'additive' colour model and is particularly important in any photographic medium where light is emitted (such as a monitor or a video display). The other colour model you will come across is a mixture of cyan, magenta and yellow – and when these are combined they create the printer's 'key' of black. Hence this 'subtractive' colour model is CMYK and is important in reflective media such as printed images.

Exhibit 6.12

The colour wheel

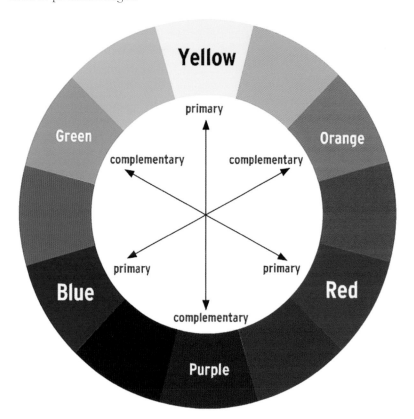

What we want to achieve is an ability to capture colours that enhance particular moods. Red is a colour we associate with aggression, danger, excitement and passion. It is the colour of the coming night. Blue is a calm colour; it tends to lower our mood, allowing us to be more reflective and absorbed in what we are seeing. It is the midday colour. Yellow is the colour of joy and vivacity – it suggests brightness and newness. Yellow is the colour of morning.

TOP TIP: If colour is really important in an image, then always shoot with the lowest ISO possible. High ISOs tend to degrade colour, particularly in the darker regions of an image.

Some colours work well together – these are referred to as complements. The golden field of corn below a deep blue sky is a great example. When two colours sit on opposite sides of the wheel, they tend to complement one another.

To build your skill and expertise you should seek to create images that exploit complementary colours using the EPF principles. For each exercise choose just one dominant colour for the shoot and work to make a feature of that colour such that it stands out and supports your point of interest in your image. Then, taking any great work of art as your inspiration, try to recreate the colours in your image. So, with Turner's masterpiece in Chapter 1, look for an opportunity in the morning light where you can capture the gorgeous reds and yellows he employed.

Exhibit 6.13
The Black Cuillins
– Bob Ryan, 2013
In this shot I created a sense of recession by varying the intensity of the 'darks' from foreground to background. The colour is muted and works using the complements of blue and orange

Robert Plutchik's work on emotion has been highly influential. Although the linkage between colour and emotion had been made before, his colour wheel gives a fascinating insight into how the two are related. Plutchik's colour wheel, although arranged slightly differently to the conventional colour wheel, portrays in two dimensions a three-dimensional, conical structure. At the base are the lighter shades of low emotional intensity and at the apex (the centre point) the pure colours representing the highest level of intensity.

Plutchik identified eight primary emotions that form four opposites, like our complementary colours:

1. joy versus sadness

2. trust versus disgust

3. fear versus anger

4. anticipation versus surprise

The wheel shows how these primary emotions relate, both through increasing or decreasing intensity and between one another. Just as mixing blue and yellow generates green, neighbouring emotions create secondary emotions, building up to the rich language we use to describe different emotional states.

Exhibit 6.14
Robert Plutchik's Wheel of Emotion
From R. Plutchik, The Nature of Emotions, *American Scientist* 89 (1980)

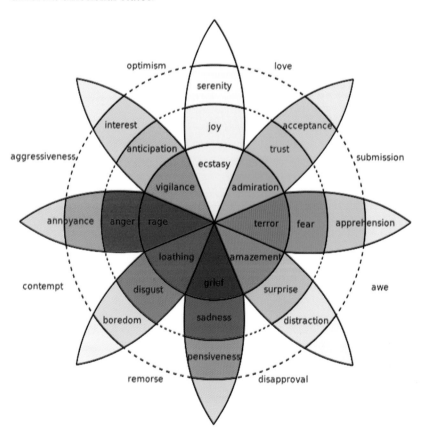

Given the powerful link between colour and emotion, the master photographer can use colour to cue a response in the viewer. Imagine a scene looking down an estuary towards a mountainous island in the far distance. We can use the vivid colours of sunset and the blue of the sea to create drama, evoking the emotions of anticipation and surprise. Alternatively, we might vary the hue of a single colour, going from high intensity in the foreground to low intensity in the far distance. This will evoke a sense of peacefulness as the viewer moves through the image to the principal point of interest. So, again, using the EPF principles and choosing music that evokes different emotions, try to capture images that reflect the colours of the mood.

Exhibit 6.15
The Alpujarra mountains, Spain
– Bob Ryan, 2015
In this image I have emphasized the continuity of colour and, by careful variation in sharpening and clarity from front to back, have created a powerful 3D effect

THE USE OF TONALITY IN MONOCHROME PHOTOGRAPHY

Contribution by Andy Beel

There is a common misconception that monochrome prints are just colour pictures minus the colour. The monochrome print does not necessarily rely on mimicking the tones and the tonal range of the original scene. Indeed, quite the reverse can be true.

Austrian photographer Josef Hoflehner makes this point in his studies of the Icelandic coast. In his work he largely disregards the mid-tones (middle greys), and relies instead on very controlled and separated highlight tones and solid blacks. This is not describing the landscape as it is but elevating it to art through the use of the black and white photographic medium and the craft of printing.

By this stage in the book you will have realized that exposure needs to be optimized, and optimized in the sense that there is useable detail recorded in the highlights. It is very important to ensure that the highlights are effectively captured and not clipped. Shadow detail can usually be recovered in post-processing.

TOP TIP: Where the dynamic range of a potential image is an issue, always expose for the highlights and process for the shadows. So that you can capture the maximum subtlety of tone, try to ensure that the histogram is centred to the right; that way the sensor is able to absorb, and the camera to process, the maximum amount of light an image can offer. But you must avoid those blinkies at all cost.

An optimally exposed digital negative gives the printer at the post-processing stage a much wider gamut of choices for the final look of the picture. A raw file is like an unprocessed negative in the days of film. It can be processed any number of different ways to create a specific look. So I repeat a point I have made before: shoot in raw, as that gives you the maximum freedom when post-processing and setting up the image for printing.

Throughout this book music is used to help stimulate our emotional state when engaged in deep practice. However, the language of music describes aspects of photography in other ways. I use the terms 'high key' and 'low key' to describe the tonality of monochrome prints. A snow scene is a good example of a high-key picture, while a night scene with subdued lighting would present us with the opportunity for a low-key shot. An optimally exposed digital negative of suitable subject matter and contrast can produce either a high-key or a low-key print, depending on how you want to interpret the result.

Print brightness and contrast can also be described in terms of major and minor keys. Prints in a major key would use the whole range of tonality or contrast available on the printing paper. In terms of print brightness, there is detailed texture in the highlights and in the shadows between 92% and 6% brightness. Where the print is made in a minor key, it will have a much reduced range of contrast and brightness; this range of brightness and contrast may be placed either at the highlight, mid-tone or shadow end of the scale. Your choice of tonality for a print will depend on your vision for your final image.

TOP TIP: When printing in either colour or black and white, you should constrain the output range to your printer. Your 'shadows with detail' should be no less than 6% brightness; where highlight texture is important, 92% brightness should be a working maximum. That way your printer (the machine) will be able to render the extremes without burnout or blocking. This can be controlled in most processing software by adjusting the contrast through the image histogram.

Lee Frost makes the point that it is not necessary to pre-visualize a monochrome outcome at the point of capture.[2] Before the digital era you would have to choose the type of film (black and white or colour), its speed, consider its best exposure, the correct filters to use and so on. With digital, the colour or black and white decision can be deferred to the point of processing and, indeed, you can choose either route.

But are there any rules for determining what will work well and what will be a disaster in black and white? Generally speaking, high-contrast images with relatively few elements, few mid-tones and a strong focal point are often worth converting. Images that rely strongly on mood, or on subtlety in shape or form, are also strong candidates for conversion. However, there is no general rule apart from one: if conversion to black

---

[2] L. Frost, Will it or Won't it?, *Black and White Photography* (The Guild of Master Craftsmen 188, April 2016).

and white simplifies the transmission of your intent when you took the image, then go for it!

One of the great joys of black and white photography is the process of printing. Generally speaking, black and white image making is best realized in print rather than through digital projection. The monochrome print takes on an additional dimension that comes from the philosophy and attitude of the printer. The printer sees the original digital negative or file as a print that has only been designed through its concept stage up to the point of image capture. All other design decisions can be taken in the various stages of post processing. Even where a photographer has a recognizable printing style, there is always a long and satisfying journey to the magic of the final print.

Photographers often argue about the role that Lightroom, Photoshop and all the other processing software programs play in modern digital photography. But it has always been the case, whether with colour or black and white, that images are taken but photographs made. The preparation and production of the digital black and white print in its post-processing stages still require the same degree of dedication, skill and experience that was vital to the darkroom exhibition print worker.

As a digital black and white printer you have choices to make about how your print will look. If you are at the beginning of learning the art and craft of printing, you may be captivated by the classic looks achieved in the darkroom by masters of the film-printing craft. These classic looks have been described as possessing an inner glow and a rich and atmospheric feel.

But the output of darkroom processes, where chemicals interacted with layers of silver salts and other light-sensitive agents, produces a qualitatively different outcome to the laying of ink on retentive papers. The latter can approximate the former but can never quite match it. This is as good a motivation as any for seeking to push the boundaries of what digital can do artistically and aesthetically through the printed medium rather than trying to emulate the output of the old ways. However, the old ways are not completely gone and if you love the look and feel of prints from the days of film you will need a dark room, a lot of interesting chemicals, specialist equipment and endless patience. But it can be done, and if that is the route this book encourages you to take in the search for greatness then go for it.

Whichever way you go, whether you print in super-saturated colour or in the most contrasted shades of black and white, take the rules of printing and then disregard them. The overriding principle is that you should use your own vision and intent to create prints that offer the viewer mood, atmosphere and an emotional connection with the subject. An expressive print, whether in colour or monochrome, delivers its impact through the emotional cues it provides to the viewer. This is an issue we will return to in the final two chapters of this book.

Exhibit 6.16

A cottage near Elgol, Isle of Skye
– 2015

This image was taken on a wet and overcast day using a hand-held point and shoot camera. The colour version has very muted colours and light but the potential for strong contrast is present in the scene. The converted image gives an uncompromising feeling of bleakness and isolation. The small stone cottage balances the waves on the foreshore creating a simple but powerful composition. A small amount of grain has also been added in post-processing

Priming Exercise 6.4

How about some inspiring and uplifting music to raise your emotional energy?

1. Take six different optimally exposed colour raw digital negatives.

2. Create two virtual copies of each negative.

3. With the first virtual copy, convert it to mono by desaturating all the colours. (Use this copy as a comparison image for the other.)

4. For the second virtual copy, stop, look and reflect on your image and write down a post-processing plan:

   - What is the subject/what do you want to dominate?

   - How are you going make the main feature dominate?

   - What needs cropping out?

   - What distractions need cloning out?

   - What needs to be lighter/ darker?

   - What needs more/less contrast?

   - What needs more/less clarity (mid-tone contrast)?

   - What needs more/less sharpening?

5. Make a mental note of the adjustments required before you start playing with your software's sliders.

6. Carry out the envisaged adjustments on the second virtual copy and compare it to the first copy. If the photographic force is with you, your vision and expression will have begun to emerge.

7. Now repeat the process in step 4 to create high-key and low key pictures of the digital negatives you have chosen. Compare all the different versions with the original. Ask yourself: what has worked and what hasn't.

TOP TIP: When post-processing, always work with virtual copies if your software allows you to do so. Leave the original raw files untouched. This gives you the scope to try different post-processing plans.

Great photography, whether at the stage of capture or at the stage of creating the final print, entails one crucial ingredient – a profound understanding of the way that your viewer will look at and appreciate the result. In Chapter 8 we return to that problem when we focus on the issue of impact. However, in Chapter 7 we focus on two issues that can help give your image making a distinct voice: creativity and narrative power.

7

STRATEGIES FOR DEVELOPING YOUR UNIQUE VOICE

'You cannot find your voice unless others hear you sing.'

– Bob Ryan

In this challenging chapter we show how the concept of deep practice can be applied to the problem of creativity and narrative. We also show the power of emulation in building skill at this level. It is well recognized in many other fields of human endeavour that emulating masterwork by looking and listening is a key approach when developing skill at this level. We stand on the shoulders of giants, and in photography that means finding great masterworks and attempting to replicate them to the best of your ability.

In this chapter we look at two constructs: creativity or self expression, and narrative. These constructs are the ways that you can express your own particular 'voice or intent' most effectively. However, as we shall see, they are often misunderstood. One common misunderstanding, as we pointed out in Chapter 3, is that 'Creative Photography' is taken as synonymous with Photoshop-generated imaginative art using and integrating elements from different images. That type of image making can be great fun and is usually fantasy based. Our concept of creativity is much broader than that. As I said in Chapter 3: creativity is about seeing the world anew and using the photographic medium in new and unanticipated ways.[1]

CREATIVITY

Creativity is often regarded as the defining characteristic of great photography. But what does it mean? For a start, it doesn't just mean original. At some level or other every image taken represents a unique view of the world. The image of two Greylag geese in flight in Chapter 5 and the image of the swan in Chapter 4 are original in the sense that they are unique to that time and place. So, creative implies more than simple originality. Perhaps by creative I mean unfamiliar – but unfamiliar to whom?

---

[1] Creative intuition is believed to operate in a different way from the problem-based intuition described in the previous chapters. An excellent article unpacking the differences and reflecting the insights in this chapter is: J. Gore and E. Sadler-Smith, Unpacking Intuition: A Process and Outcome Framework, *Review of General Psychology* 15 (2011), 304–16.

Is it unfamiliar to the ordinary man or woman in the street, or to a picture editor working for one of the major photographic magazines or a Royal Photographic Society assessor examining distinction candidates?

John Szarkowski, the former Curator of the New York Museum of Modern Art, came up with a description of the range of creative possibilities in the 1970s. All photographers, he suggested, express their voice or intent on a continuum between a window at one extreme and a mirror at the other. A 'window', according to Szarkowski, is a photographer whose intent is to look and truthfully record the world exactly as it is with as little personal interpretation as possible. Windows see themselves as ciphers for an external reality at which they just happened to be pointing their camera. The reason why the photographer should choose to take a particular image is, of course, subjective, but for the window what is recorded in the camera is objective truth.

A mirror, on the other hand, is at the other end of the creative and expressive continuum. For this the photographer creates an image that allows them to interpret the scene in front of the camera. The fidelity of the end result is not what matters – the reality of the image is the end result, no more, no less. In this we see a reflection of Adam's story in Chapter 2. For Adam, the image was a product of his own mind; reality was a product of his own internal, mental world.

Finding your creative space

The problem with continuums – whether we split the world of photography into 'empiricists' and 'rationalists', 'realists' and 'idealists' or, indeed, 'windows' and 'mirrors' – is that they destroy subtlety for the sake of simplicity. What are we to make of the image of the waterfall in Exhibit 7.1? At which end of the window–mirror spectrum does an image lie that asks us to explore the way we see and interpret chaos and uncertainty? What level of our perception of reality does the face in the falls reflect?[2] The key to creativity is the willingness to transcend stereotypes and, in terms of what we are saying here, continuums.

---

[2] With this image I allow the viewer to experience their own reaction to chaos and uncertainty. When confronted in this way, the viewer's non-conscious mind will attempt to impose structure and meaning on what they see. This is the effect that allows us to see the face of a man in the moon or a religious icon in the Arctic ice. The phenomenon he is investigating is pareidolia, and with this he is allowing us to reflect on the workings of our minds.

When we were young we may have pointed our cameras at the world we saw and been happy with the result. For many, that is as far as they ever want to go. For others, their journey reflects what they see done by others – photography has waves of fashion – but the great photographer looks for their own space, not on a continuum but outside it. Through their work they define new creative possibilities.

As you think more and more about your preferred 'creative space' your brain will start the process of priming the insights necessary to achieve the outcomes you want. This stage of preparation and 'incubation' is very important and explains the common observation amongst photographers that they never get their best shots on their first visit to a location. The priming exercises in this chapter are designed to help you incubate the creative process.

Exhibit 7.1

Pareidolia – the devil in the falls

– Bob Ryan, 2016

In this shot I have taken an image at the foot of a waterfall in Skye. However, my intention was not to photograph a waterfall but to present an image that makes us think about our own mental reaction to chaos and turbulence

Priming Exercise 7.1

Take 20 of your most recent images and, using no more than six words that make sense as a whole, express your feelings about each. Now, looking at each description, put the images into no more than five clusters and then, in six words, describe your feelings about each cluster. Finally, put them all together and find another six words that sum them all up. The six-word limit is a terrific discipline for helping you to think hard about what you are looking at.

Definitions of creativity

So now, what do we mean by the term creative? The idea of creativity incorporates the notion of 'imagination' – we do not see the world as it really is; we see it as we imagine it is. Our ability to translate how we view the world into art is an important part of the creative process. Creativity also entails a purpose or the fulfilment of an objective and through that it derives its value. It is, as I have already said, a mistake to think of creativity as synonymous with originality. Originality is a relative construct. What the ordinary viewer perceives as original is unlikely to be regarded as such by the expert photographer, photographic analyst or assessor. The reverse is true in that what the specialists in many artistic fields regard as good would leave the ordinary viewer cold and uninspired.

Creativity has been described as the 'Divine Spark' – a phrase that captures the essence of the sudden and the spontaneous. Some images have the ability to transform the viewer's perception instantly – as when I first saw Salgado's 'City of Ice', as related in Chapter 3. So creative art is 'transformative' in that it captures the mind of the viewer and takes them to another place. We will return to this final element in the creative act in Chapter 8.

So, creativity is a relative construct – creativity is that inspired blend of originality, imagination and divine spark that puts you at the door of greatness.

If you have been successful in your journey so far, you will have all the technical skills and knowledge to take your photography to a new creative level. Indeed, those skills and knowledge are now part of your mental firmware to the point that when you look through the viewfinder, the camera has dissolved as an instrument intervening between you and your intended image. So, given that happy state, what strategies can be employed to push your creative boundaries?

The exercises at the end of this discussion of creativity are designed to do just that – to help you build the creative side of your work. One thread through many of them is learning through emulation. It is well recognized in many creative disciplines – music, literature, painting and sports like tennis and golf – that focused copying of how others perform is an indispensable strategy for enhancing your own expertise and creative power. We excel by standing on the shoulders of giants, so if you see a great photographer lining up to take a shot, make sure you get it too. If you go on a photographic course and the course leader starts taking photographs, ask and then copy what they do.

Creativity and the talent myth

Have you ever seen Michelangelo's painting *The Creation*, adorning the ceiling of the Sistine Chapel in Rome? It depicts, as its central motif, the moment that Adam receives the 'Divine Spark' from God. Perhaps before the Age of Enlightenment the divine spark was an obvious way of thinking about the initiation of ideas. Now we understand that creativity or self-expression does not happen quite like that.

Exhibit 7.2
***The Creation of Adam*, the Sistine Chapel**
Is this what creativity is about?

Those who are blessed with what we call talent do not receive ideas ready formed from heaven in a flash.[3] As noted in the introduction to this book: to become good or great at any human endeavour requires

[3] See A. Koestler, *The Act of Creation* (Basingstoke: Pan Books, 1975). This book gives an interesting perspective on spontaneity and intuition in the process of creative thought. Koestler's work is very consistent with that of Gore and Sadler-Smith, 'Unpacking Intuition' (see p. 94, n.1).

commitment and practice. Talent is the product of both. There is no 'talent gene' – decades of research into the psychology of excellence demonstrate that. There are no easy shortcuts to consistently producing work of a high calibre, but I suspect you have absorbed that idea already and begun to prove it to yourself following the advice I have given so far.

Are there lucky, gifted individuals who have all the photographic talent, or do they just work harder than the rest of us? There is a feeling expressed by many photographers that there are those with a natural talent and aptitude for creative or expressive photography. The rest of us are left to struggle with either the artistic and or the technical side of the medium. The good news is that if you have the drive and commitment to apply yourself to learning the EPF process, you can make huge steps in any photographic direction you choose.

Invest your time and energy in those activities that are important but not necessarily urgent in developing your self-expression. It's easy to let the important directional thinking like dreams, hopes and goals get lost in the mayhem of daily life. Many studies have shown that those who are most driven or passionate about the goals they set for themselves win in the end.[4]

Brett is a retired technology and design lecturer who approached Andy looking for help with his application for Associateship of the Royal Photographic Society. This distinction is a goal that many photographers aspire to. He had already achieved the first level distinction (Licentiateship) and had subsequently developed an interest in making books about the work of local artisans. Brett's first idea was based around the workings of a pottery near where he lived, and the idea he had for his 'A' panel was a linear progression of 15 images from preparation of the clay to the finished pot.

Andy asked Brett to focus on Stephen Covey's second habit: 'begin with the end in mind'.[5] They discussed the use and the location of pottery products when they are with their eventual owners, and worked back from there. They also discussed the relationships between the potter and his clients, and the potter and the clay provider at the local brickworks.

[4]   Two references covering the topic of 'talent' are G. Klein, *Seeing What Others Don't: The Remarkable Ways We Gain Insights* (London: Nicholas Brealey Publishing, 2013) and G. Colvin, *Talent is Overrated* (London: Nicholas Brealey Publishing, 2010).
[5]   S. Covey, *The Seven Habits of Highly Successful People* (New York: Simon and Schuster, 1974).

CREATIVITY AS A PROCESS

Contribution by Andy Beel

The creative process is a method of collecting ideas and insights, thinking about relationships between the ideas, and weeding out weak and unhelpful aspects that do not add to the theme or objective. There is the potential for any project of any type or size to fail because the original brief or idea was not fully thought through. The project runs out of time and/or money before completion – sounds familiar, doesn't it? How is this related to photography?

Photography projects fail because a single idea is followed through without testing the idea thoroughly first. In my work coaching photography, I come across many people seeking photographic distinctions. My primary task is to inspire a far greater diversity of thought by the applicant about what the panel of pictures they intend to submit is about.

The storyboard that Brett had prepared for his original idea was expanded to create a photographic project that would be of interest to a wider audience than students of pottery. The benefit of discussing ideas and relationships with others is that it expands the possibility of what can be achieved. No one person knows everything or necessarily thinks the same way as somebody else.

THE CREATIVITY FUNNEL – FOUR Ss

Contribution by Andy Beel

We can think of the generation and filtering of ideas as being like using a sieve that progressively catches smaller and smaller rocks until only fine soil remains.

Using the sieve idea, select the photographers you want to study in depth in the exercise overleaf.

Priming Exercise 7.2

Contribution by Andy Beel

1. Sieve and Select: Choose three photographers whose work you love and wish to emulate.

2. Study: the work of your three selected photographers until you understand their vision, intent and emotional cues.

3. Steal: choose a favourite picture from each of your chosen photographers and emulate it as best you can.

4. Synthesize the vision, intent, style, way of seeing and emotional cues of all three photographers in your work. The idea is not to copy their work but to combine those elements together into your own images.

5. In your own work, use the ideas and insight gained from this extended study to change the emphasis of what you intend and capture. Get ideas about what you should omit, include and transform in your image taking and then remix them. David Bowie, a highly original and influential musician who died in 2016, used to take newspapers and chop them into bits, remixing them as he searched for new ideas. Try that with your images, mentally cutting, pasting and reworking the ideas behind them.

Creativity is a process that can be learned by anybody. It is as natural as breathing the fresh air or warming yourself in the sun. As an adult, your brain is about 3 pounds in weight and has approximately 86 billion neurons, the tiny cells that perform its basic functioning. There is enough computational power in a single brain to hold all the books ever printed, 40 times over. It does creativity, it just does – all you have to do is let it.

Here are a few pointers to help create and prioritize your ideas

- Who or what inspires you – whose work or style do you really love?

- What multiple threads are you going to borrow from whom? Use the four Ss of the creative sieve above to help you.

- Decide on a theme.

- Think about the outline of your intent: what do you want to say with your voice, whether it is expressive or narrative? Write it down.

- Collect your ideas and write them down; perhaps use your phone camera as a scrapbook.

- Create a folder for borrowed ideas and snippets you might like to remix later.

- Filter and test your ideas with the following in mind:
    - Is it visually interesting?
    - Is it interesting to others?
    - Do you know enough about the subject?
    - Is it practically possible?
    - What resources in terms of time and money will be required?
    - Do you have anything new or different to say photographically?

- Think about the interrelationships between your differing ideas.

- Put the project aside for a while and let your non-conscious mind work to find interrelationships and connections between different ideas.

- Re-evaluate where you are and what potential outcomes there could be; add or omit ideas that are outside the scope of what you are trying to achieve.

- Narrow down the number of possibilities to two or three that have the most potential.

- Make up a storyboard to plan a panel of prints – what are the must have shots? Write in the variety of possible approaches, focal lengths, apertures and so on.

- Prepare a shooting list based on the storyboard ideas.

- Begin taking pictures for those ideas that you believe have the most potential.

- Review and evaluate those that have the strongest potential to go all the way to achieving the intent you had when you started.

- Fully complete this last, combined, strongest idea with all its twists, turns and changes. Very probably you will now be in a completely different place to where you first started.

Exhibit 7.3
St Mary's Churchyard, Painswick,
Gloucestershire, 2014
The influences for this picture and
those of a similar style in Andy's
portfolio are taken from the work
of Bill Brandt, Brassai and the Lith
printing process

Can creativity become a habit?

Yes, it can. Read the book by Twyla Tharp called *The Creative Habit –*
Learn and Use it for Life,[6] written by a highly influential choreographer
with 18 honorary doctorates to her name.

---

[6]   T. Tharp, *The Creative Habit – Learn and Use it for Life* (New York: Simon and
Schuster, 2007).

Tharp's book takes the reader through the old-fashioned virtues of routine, perseverance, discipline, preparation, risk-taking and regular self-assessment. These characteristics are applicable to any creative or artistic endeavour, so please don't be put off reading this book because it was not written by a photographer. We all have things to learn from other creative mediums.

TOP TIP: To reinforce the point, wherever you see great art or great artists at work, ask what it is they see and if they mind if you take a shot as well. A word of explanation often helps, and a promise not to use the shot commercially or in competition will also help. If you go on a photographic course, ask to see what the course leader sees and take the shot.

Now, here are some exercises designed to use the EPF and emulation techniques to build your creative skill.

1. Select and review your top ten images. Read your notes in your photographic journal and then ask for each image:

    (i) What was original about this image?

    (ii) How did it differ from the majority of my other images?

    (iii) What special technical skill did it employ (light, colour, composition, etc.)?

2. With those ten images and where feasible, retake the image but vary the capture elements: focus, exposure, depth of field, use of light, colour. See also if you can improve the composition. Don't forget the inspiring music, and to check and review as quickly as you can.

3. This is an excellent exercise in building your creative intent: with a location or potential image in mind, draw a sketch of what it is you would like to take. Work out, in the sketch, the overall composition and where the principal points of interest would lie. Make a note of how you would emphasize them. Then go out and take the shot.

4. Find some of the very best images in a genre you enjoy, either in magazines or books. Cut out or copy those images into your journal and then seek to reproduce the image as closely as you can.

Process the images to the same standard and only stop when you are happy you have achieved a superior image.

5. Find an image of an old master painting in a genre that strongly appeals to you. Make a detailed sketch of the painting, analysing it as you would a photograph. Then attempt to recreate that painting photographically.

6. With just one lens (a 50mm prime is a good choice to start with) go to a favourite location and take 100 shots. For wildlife shooters this works well with a 300mm prime or similar. Then switch off the autofocus, deliberately put the camera out of focus and take another 100 shots. Repeat with AF on but at (say) 1/20th of a second.

7. Using a story of your choosing (perhaps from a novel, short story or poem), prepare a panel of three images that reflect the key elements of that story.

So you want to maximize your creativity? Here is a list of guiding principles:

1. Be clear about your photographic intent but not obsessively so – be prepared to go with the opportunities that present themselves.

2. Clear your mind, find your own space and centre yourself. Through music and/or storytelling clear your mind of your daily concerns. There is a lot of evidence that a positive frame of mind boosts creativity,[7] while negativity kills it and reverts you to that System 2 thinking described in Chapters 1 and 2. So, get positive!

3. Look through the camera, with the emphasis on through. Forget it's there. By this stage of your journey the essential competencies are burnt in and its presence should now be beginning to dissolve in your awareness.

---

[7] Gore and Sadler-Smith, 'Unpacking Intuition' (see p. 94, n.1).

4. Believe in yourself. 'To your own self be true', as Shakespeare said. Do not worry about your ability to be creative or harbour any sense that you lack talent. Performance anxiety – as psychologists refer to it – is the death of creativity.

5. Let your intuitive mind run riot. Take photographic risks (I do not advocate physical ones). Ask yourself what is unusual in the image possibilities in front of you and explore them.

6. Look for contradictions and ambiguities in the subject you plan to take. Often, as Arthur Koestler suggested, it is when quite different aspects of a problem clash that the moment of creation comes.

7. What we see as ordinary, others see as creative and inspiring – exhibit your images, compete in competitions, submit your work for publication and welcome and absorb all the feedback you can. You cannot find your voice unless others hear you sing.

You may have noticed in your photography how the local area where you live looks so uninteresting and ordinary. But to others from far away it is exciting and novel. When you look at your own images you may think they are uninteresting and lacking in creativity. Maybe Michelangelo had doubts about his own ability as he hung upside down painting the fresco that adorns the ceiling of the Sistine Chapel – we will never know. But rest assured, as your intuitive mind begins to create, others will recognize it – often before you do.

BUILDING NARRATIVE

Narrative is the art of relating events and telling of the connection between them. In literature a narrative is likely to have the following elements: exposition, conflict, climax and resolution. Narrative therefore implies a flow of events, but photography does not have an explicit time dimension. It 'freezes a moment' but, with the clues it provides, the viewer can reconstruct the history and the future the image implies.

Take, for example, the Pulitzer Prize-winning image from the Vietnam War in which a young girl has been horribly burned by a misdirected napalm attack (Exhibit 7.4). The image had a profound impact upon the American psyche and the attitude of the American people to the war.

The narrative is straightforward: war is raging behind the young children and they are running in pain and terror. The young girl is running naked and screaming, trying to catch up with the boy in front. The image can be read at many levels, but its power still shocks decades after the event.

Exhibit 7.4
South Vietnamese forces follow after terrified children, including 9-year-old Kim Phuc
– Nick Ut/AP/Press Association Images
This dramatic image of a young girl and her family running from a napalm attack in the Vietnam War shocked the world

In photography, narrative strength is enhanced by a number of different elements, all of which should be present to some degree:

- A context: any narrative arises from a sequence of events that have a cause and a potential conclusion. The context in which a photographic narrative sits should be readily implied within the image. In Exhibit 7.5 I show a cheetah cub about to kill a fleeing baby antelope. From the image we can recognize, but not be distracted by, the open grassland in which the event occurs. It is also possible to tell from the height of the grass and the size of the animals that they are both very young. Through tight composition I have removed unnecessary detail from the shot. The central positioning within the frame focuses our attention on the action and the skilled use of depth of field reveals the context and colours of the savannah.

- A dynamic: the image should imply movement and change. The image of the Generalife (Exhibit 6.2) has no dynamic element apart from the frozen movement of water from the fountains. It has no narrative power. The image of the cheetah just about to bury its teeth into the neck of its prey has a dynamic, and the viewer can imagine what preceded the moment (the chase) and what followed (the kill).

- An emotional connection: we discuss the problem of communicating emotion in more detail in Chapter 8. However, unless there is an emotional connection the viewer is unlikely to bother to read an image's narrative intent. Where emotions are in conflict the narrative will be enhanced. In the image of the cheetah about to kill, we respond through the cues in the image to the terror experienced by the prey. The cues are there in the eyes and the straining sinews. However, there are also emotions in conflict: the prey is showing its terror, the young cheetah its elation at the imminent accomplishment of its kill.

- A relationship: narrative strength is increased when there is a clear visual connection between elements within the image. Although the elements are frozen in the moment, strong composition and all the other qualities of good image making described in the previous chapters come together to enhance the connections within the image.

- A decisive moment: in any sequence of events there is a moment where the past and the future are realized most perfectly in the present. The decisive moment is associated with the climax of the narrative. Usually it is just that moment, the instant before the climax. In the cheetah kill a number of shots were taken just before and just after the event shown. Why is the event shown the decisive moment? The viewer can read the sense of movement and interpret that we are at the end of a chase. The jaws descending on the neck and the bared teeth forewarn of what will certainly happen and the viewer is in no doubt about the outcome.

Exhibit 7.5

A cheetah kill

– Bob Ryan, 2011

This moment in the takedown of the kill has both impact and narrative power. We can guess what led to the moment and we are certain what the outcome will be. It is in the prelude to climax that the critical moment is found

Great photography is about being able to recognize these elements in a potential image intuitively. There are two stages to this process: learning to recognize narrative power within an image and learning to recognize the narrative potential within any given situation.

To achieve the first, you should rework all of your images within your journal for narrative power, perhaps scoring them against the quintet of context, dynamic, emotion, relationship and decisive moment.

For example, in Exhibit 7.6 we can easily read a very funny story: a wild dog has come across a rhinoceros. Wild dogs, like all dogs, are very playful animals, particularly when they have just fed. Playful is not how we would describe rhinos. Wild dogs are also relatively small, whilst rhinos are very big. These two animals have come face to face by accident. This image is unusual in two ways: firstly, the rhino and the wild dog are two of the rarest of South Africa's animals, and to get both in the same shot is quite exceptional. Secondly, the moment has been caught where the two animals are connected – they are sizing one another up, and in nature it is rare for animals to make and sustain eye contact with one another for more than a second or two. What is the likely outcome? The wild dog thinks better of it and scampers away, or it stands its ground and the rhino turns and makes chase. The humour is in the David and Goliath moment – a story that has been told over and over again but which often has us rooting for the little guy.

Exhibit 7.6
Wild dog and rhino, South Africa
– Bob Ryan, 2011

By this stage you have burnt all the basic and transformational skills into your brain, and following the EPF principles you are able to respond to a situation instantly. Now, using those same principles, identify opportunities where events are happening and where you can take images freely. The world around you is teeming with stories, and any busy street scene or other place where events are being acted out provides the potential for narrative. If your genre is landscape, look for narrative in the rural scene – the story an image tells does not need to be complex or highly dramatic. Indeed, simplicity in narrative is often a virtue. So now, a test of your photographic skill:

- Go out with a companion or two on a bright, moonlit night with your camera and a standard lens. Work the streets of your local town or village, looking for small happenings – people getting on or off buses, coming out of the local pub or church, popping into the all-night store – all provide great subjects for narrative photography.

- Rework the above exercise on a night when there is no moon, possibly with rain or snow depending on the time of year.

- Go along to an outdoor event such as a sack race, steam rally or carnival and look for stories being acted out.

With both creativity and narrative, continuous deep practice using the principles will bring its rewards. As you continue to practise you will begin to understand and anticipate events and their photographic significance. Watch carefully what other photographers are looking at and photographing. Don't try to prejudge whether they are better photographers than you – just look at what they are seeing and make your own judgement. Additionally, when you are with a crowd, make careful notes of what others are looking and pointing at. You never know, it might be Superman coming to save the world and you could have the scoop of a lifetime (OK – I know he doesn't really exist, but hopefully you get the point). This process of peer observation has two very useful attributes: firstly, you gain skill in seeing through copying and secondly, you do begin to understand, at an intuitive level, what attracts others.

Those who really master the art of personal photography make intuitive judgements about the value of the work they see others producing and how it may be rethought and reinterpreted in their own style. Those who follow the crowd, live and work like the crowd. Have faith in your creative and imaginative abilities and resist being sucked in to the blandness of the mass media. Give yourself permission to be the photographer you are, not a poor imitation of somebody else.

So now, are you ready? Let's go on to the final level in our journey and explore how we can give our images impact – the sort of impact that changes the way you see the world.

Exhibit 7.7

9/11

– Bob Ryan, 2015

Out of context, this image, whilst evocative, does not have narrative power until you read the title. Once you see that, you immediately begin to fill in the back story of loss and love represented by a rose placed on a name. Note also how the rose has its own internal light, which helps cue your own emotional response to the image

8

THE ROUTE TO
IMPACT

Developing impact in photography, it is said, is the one skill that cannot be taught. That is not true. To deliver impact we need to make a radical change in our attitude to photography and recognize that what we photograph isn't what we see but what we feel. The photographer Arnold Newman said: 'We do not take pictures with our cameras but with our hearts and minds.' The camera is only a means to that end.

Our route to impact is, in part, building upon the body of skills and expertise developed so far on our journey. However, impact is much more than just those skills and expertise. It represents the most immediate and powerful emotional connection with the viewer. It entails an understanding of what has impact for you as the photographer and for your potential viewer.

Impact is about delivering emotional intensity in our image making. All the constructs so far have been about setting the scene for this most important area of photographic judgement. To achieve this, you need to be able to 'burn in' to your brain the ability to instantly:

(1)   Recognize the potential picture

(2)   Recognize the moment of peak emotional impact in an image, and crucially;

(3)   Know how to communicate that moment to the eventual viewer.

Impact therefore combines both intent and outcome: what emotional response do you wish to induce in the viewer and how do you achieve it?

But before we get carried away: what is emotion? One thing it is not is 'emoting', nor is it sentimentality. Emotion is the depth of feeling you have when you respond to some external or mental stimulus or 'cue'. Physiologically, emotion is the automatic response of your body's 'sympathetic nervous system' to cues that trigger unconscious brain activity controlling your heart rate, blood pressure and the secretion of various hormones that influence your mood. Emotion can be as varied as joy, rage, contentment, anger, jealousy, fear and all the colours in between – note the use of the word 'colour', and think back to Chapter 6 and Plutchik's colour wheel. But emotion can be also be portrayed through the use of contrast, the use of light and indeed all of the intuitive expertise you have developed so far.

At its most neutral, an image must have the potential to surprise, to reveal to the viewer something about the world that they did not know. If someone has not seen a black swan, then an image of a black swan will show that they exist and what they look like. This is using photography as a means of factual communication. This is the image working at the 'phenomenal' level. We are seeing something we did not know existed and we can marvel at the beauty of this particular type of swan. Now imagine a photograph of a black swan taking off majestically through the morning mist lit by shafts of golden light from the newly risen sun. That has greater surprise value and it will have greater impact. In this case the image is working at the ontological level by revealing an element of the underlying reality of the swan in its natural world at its most beautiful.

To have impact on a viewer an image must penetrate to the heart of how the viewer thinks and, most importantly, feels about what is represented. Achieving impact is about creating the conditions that lift the ordinary to the extraordinary from the viewers' point of view. For example, a picture of a steam locomotive taken on a bright, sunny day will have less emotional impact than a shot of the same locomotive taken at dawn in a grimy maintenance shed. The shafts of early morning light come streaming through the soot-caked skylights, with deep and mysterious shadows created by the engine's wafting steam and smoke providing atmosphere as the driver and fireman oil the wheel bearings in preparation for the day's hard and dirty work. Merely describing the image this way gives a clue as to the source of the impact. Steam and smoke, shadows and shafts of light are all cues that evoke a sense of mystery and raise the emotional intensity experienced by the viewer. As we become more familiar with a subject we discover the untapped cues that can be explored and captured to enhance impact.

There are, in summary, three levels at which we respond to images:

1. The *phenomenal*, being recognition of what the image actually is – the subject matter. When we see something unfamiliar, we react to it; it stimulates our curiosity and wonder. This is the level of impact that the 'window' described in Chapter 7 can hope to achieve.

2. The *ontological*, being recognition of the underlying reality that the image represents. All that we see and experience has a context and wider reality. An image of a figure walking down a road can, in Andy's hands, reveal the mood and the loneliness of the figure in a stark and uncompromising world. Here, he is exploring through his camera and through post processing a deeper level of reality – he is working at an ontological level.

3. The *existential*, where an image shifts our understanding of our own relationship with what the image represents. Some images have such power that they shift our consciousness and in a moment we see the world quite differently. In Chapter 1 we focused on Alison's photograph of the dying orang-utan baby. In that image she has captured the poignancy of a mother unable to help her child, and with it the fragility of nature. No further explanation is required.

Exhibit 8.1
Elephant bath time, India
– Bob Ryan, 2015
The impact of this image is in the nature of what is being done to the animal and represents the precariousness of the handler's position, both in how he is balanced but also in his size compared to that of the elephant he is washing at the end of the day's work. At what level does the image have impact? What are the cues it is communicating to you?

So, to deliver impact you need to be clear about the type and strength of your own emotional response to a scene and then visualize how you can communicate that response to your viewer. As we have said before: if an image doesn't do anything for you, it will do nothing for your viewer.

Much is said about pre-visualization – a term that many masters of the art use to describe a key step in their approach. The difficulty is that they are coming at it from the perspective of the *visual* arts. They believe that what they are photographing and communicating is what they see, but the reality is quite different. What they are communicating is what they 'feel'. When we considered creativity or expression and narrative in Chapter 7, we focused on the nature of the message – how to be original in what we photograph and how to tell the story. But does the viewer of the image know what is creative, or can they interpret the narrative the image conveys – or, indeed, do they care?

The answer is probably 'no' unless we can engage a higher level of connection with our viewer. This connection is achieved when we release, in them, an emotional response. This higher level of connection is 'impact', and we obtain it by recognizing and capturing visual 'cues'.

As we saw when we looked at the colour wheel in Chapter 6, we are all capable of a wide variety of emotional states and in order to generate impact we need to do two things: inject emotional intensity into our image making and provide a range of visual cues that will evoke that same emotional intensity in our viewer. If you have followed our learning strategy so far you will be familiar with the use of music as an emotional cue. Music is extremely powerful but so are tangible objects, events, movements and sensations. We can use these to help intensify our emotional response to a given situation and in so doing bring all the non-conscious constructs into play.

Alison was in a safari truck with her camera and a 70–200 lens attached. It was a bright morning and she had been watching a female cheetah and her cubs playing around a group of safari vehicles parked some 50 metres away. She had her camera set in aperture priority, ISO 400 and at f5.6. Her vibration reduction was active and she had the in-camera metering set at 'matrix'. After a while the cheetah family started walking away from the group and towards her truck. The light was strong but the sun still relatively low in the sky. She sensed that some good shots of the young cubs might be coming her way but was quite unprepared for what happened next. The lead cub had disturbed a newborn eland antelope, stranded in a small thicket when its mother ran from the approaching cheetahs. The eland burst out of the thicket and the eldest cub, followed by its siblings, gave chase, brought down and killed the stricken animal. Alison reacted to the scene instantly, dropped to a crouch, steadied her camera and took a sequence of breathtaking shots in the 14 seconds between the first moment of the disturbance and the final kill. Every shot was technically of a high standard but the culminating shot, when her own emotional intensity was at a peak, is the one that delivers the highest impact. Now, whenever she photographs an animal, the mere physical act of dropping to a crouching position and bringing the camera to her eye cues the intense excitement and concentration she felt that morning in the Masai Mara.

TOP TIP: A key step in activating any given emotional state is to create a cue that will help you associate a particular context with a given emotional state. Your personal cue may be physical, aural – as with music – or visual. What matters is: can you reproduce it when you need it?

Repeating the cue every time you seek images in that type of context will progressively enhance your emotional response, and as you do so you will find that all nine of the subordinate constructs will come into play. You will not be aware that your non-conscious brain has taken control of your image making and you are intuitively recognizing and capturing impact.

To begin developing this level of expertise, reflect upon your personal top five events or situations that have produced a powerful emotional response in you over the last 12 months. They need to be visual events that you have witnessed. Here are my and Andy Beel's top five lists:

Bob:

- Seeing a crocodile taking down a zebra in the Masai Mara river crossing (cue: struggle, churning)

- Watching a flock of swans coming in to land on a lake at Slimbridge (cue: dark, ominous sky)

- The church spire at Tetbury lit up with mist swirling around (cue: separation of elements by mist, mix of contrast)

- Gazing upon the Cuillin Hills, Skye (cue: black, strong light, jagged and fractured skyline)

- Walking close to the head of Niagara Falls in Canada (cue: power of movement, folding, precipitous drop)

Andy:

- Taking pictures in Millennium Square, Bristol (cue: brightness against dark subject/light background)

- Taking pictures in Sussex near Emsworth (cue: diagonal light leading the eye to the top right)

- Taking images of tools and machinery in my late father's workshop (cue: strong directional light, shadows, cobwebs)

- Kimmeridge Bay – taking a shot of this famous location (cue: tank traps as a foreground, tower on the headland)

- Images of the Snowdonia Horseshoe (cue: dark, moody sky, windy, light constantly changing)

Whenever you have an intense emotional experience while taking an image, make a note of the location and the cues, identify the colour of the emotion, note the extent of your activation and the degree of your feeling (pleasant to unpleasant). Note these details on the acquired images in your journal.

Location	Intent	Music	Colour	Emotion	Cue

As you progress, certain types of image making will become associated in your mind with a given emotional response. As you seek images of that type, using the EPF technique, you will discover that you begin, naturally and without effort, to identify shots that have the stronger emotional resonance for you. As you focus, set your exposure, select the best depth of field, capture the best light and so on, your sympathetic system will begin to respond automatically as the most appropriate choices are made.

Now, with each one, try to identify which emotion dominated your feelings at the time and the cue that activated your response. For example, when I go out on a cold and clear night the memory of the northern lights flickering across the sky comes vividly back, including the feeling of awe that I felt at the time. The sense of awe was my emotional response but the cue is feeling the frosty chill of a dark night when the stars are out and all is quiet. As we look at the colour wheel we see the feeling of awe sits between its two associated colours of green and blue, and these are, indeed, the dominant colours associated with the northern lights.

By identifying the cue and activating the emotional response you will intensify your search for impact in your image making. So, the strategy for developing impact is as follows:

1. **Think through your photographic intent. In doing so, focus not only on the image you want to take but, more importantly, the emotion you want to communicate.**

2. Look through your journal for images that created in you feelings you want to capture again, noting the music that you used at the time and other relevant shooting data. Note in particular the likely cues that could bring that emotion to the fore.

3. As you approach the shoot, recollect the most appropriate cue. Think about what was uniquely attributable to the previous occasions when you experienced that emotion whilst out with your camera.

4. Find a way to reactivate the cue and, with your music playing, relax into the moment. Check through your camera settings, look through the viewfinder – look for the colours, the light, the patterns and the contrast that reflect that emotion.

5. Pay attention to the emotional cue in the images you are taking – the dominant cue may well form your principal point of interest and will almost certainly need emphasis in post-processing.

Tony loved photographing old churches and churchyards, but he could never quite translate into his images the sense of timelessness and peace that he felt when he walked around the neat gardens and between the stones. So he decided to try the EPF principles, and to help engage his emotions he also loaded his portable music player with a small selection of tracks that he associated with the church. One piece was the climax of Elgar's 'The Dream of Gerontius', where the soul of Gerontius enters the Judgement Hall and comes face to face with God. Even before he began the job of post-processing, the images he had taken possessed power and emotional intensity. Focusing on that intensity, he noticed a number of shapes and contrasts that lifted his images above the ordinary. These were the cues he emphasized in his post-processing and when he printed the images they elicited a similar and powerful response in those who saw them.

What Tony was seeing was very familiar to him but by linking his surroundings with powerful and relevant music, he was able to translate his emotional energy into imagery. His subsequent processing gave him the opportunity to reflect on those aspects of the images that stimulated his response and how to enhance them selectively. In this he discovered an important fact in photography – when seeking impact, we look for the cues that stimulate the emotion we intend to invoke. It is these cues, whether they be colours, light, contrast or a particular aspect of the image, that have the power, for the overwhelming number of people, of triggering an emotional response.

> *I was on a long-haul flight with a copy of* Black and White Photographer *on my knee. Don McCullin's image of the 'Shell-Shocked Marine' was on the cover. An air steward stopped and said that she had always loved that image. Intrigued, I asked why. 'It's the eyes', she said, 'they say it all and I often wondered what happened to him.' She was right, of course – she saw what Don McCullin had seen nearly 50 years previously. The cue was in the eyes.*

Alison was awestruck by the majesty of Niagara Falls. Staying on the Canadian side, she decided to try to get some close-up images of the falls, capturing the sense of awe and vulnerability she continued to feel whenever she walked down to view them at close quarters. What she decided was the best place to view the falls was from one of the two paddle steamers that took tourists close into the bottom of the falls. Here, with an upward shot, she was sure she would be able to capture that overwhelming sense of raw natural power that the falls evoked. She had on her music player dramatic music that heightened the emotional intensity of the scene as she approached the huge plume of spray thrown up by the cascading water, so much so that she stayed by the guardrail of the boat with the water drenching every part of her not covered by the flimsy plastic cagoule given to every passenger by the boat operator. She took a short sequence of shots of which one stood out, and as soon as she was able she downloaded the shot and made notes in her journal of what she felt and what cued her feelings as she took the shot.

When home and returning to post-processing, she played the music again and was soon absorbed in the process of bringing to the fore those elements of the image that activated her emotional reaction to the falls. She made some quick decisions:

1. **The perspective of the shot added to its drama, so ensuring that the height of the falls dominated the composition was crucial. She decided, through the processing, to emphasize depth and height in the image. These were important cues for her.**

2. The presence of colour in the image detracted from the appreciation of the stark contrast between the darkness of the rocks and the whiteness of the cascade. So she decided that the image would be best represented in black and white.

3. The small element of sky and the dark rocks framing the image would enhance the sense of brooding within the image. The strong contrasts were an important cue for her and she would work on them.

Exhibit 8.2
Niagara Falls
– Alison Price, 2015
The drama of the falls is captured by the perspective, the sense of movement and of scale. As we look down at Alison's image, we can almost sense the thunder of the water crashing down and the screeching of the gulls as they wheel in the mist

4. The wheeling birds low in the frame enhanced the sense of perspective and the scale of the falls but also, crucially, the vulnerability she felt. So she decided that the birds should be a dominant motif in the lower part of the image.

5. Finally, the light within the image had both intensity and luminosity – this cued the sense of drama within the image and brought it to life.

So, impact is about the capture of the cues that trigger the emotional response you feel when you press the shutter and, indeed, when you look again at the raw image on your computer. But where to now? This isn't the end of the story and in the next chapter – as we draw our journey to a close – we will summarize what we believe are key points on the method of learning described in this book.

Exhibit 8.3
Scheveningen Harbour, the
Netherlands, September 2013
– Andy Beel
Emotional cues – twilight, light and shadow, human interest, ambiguity

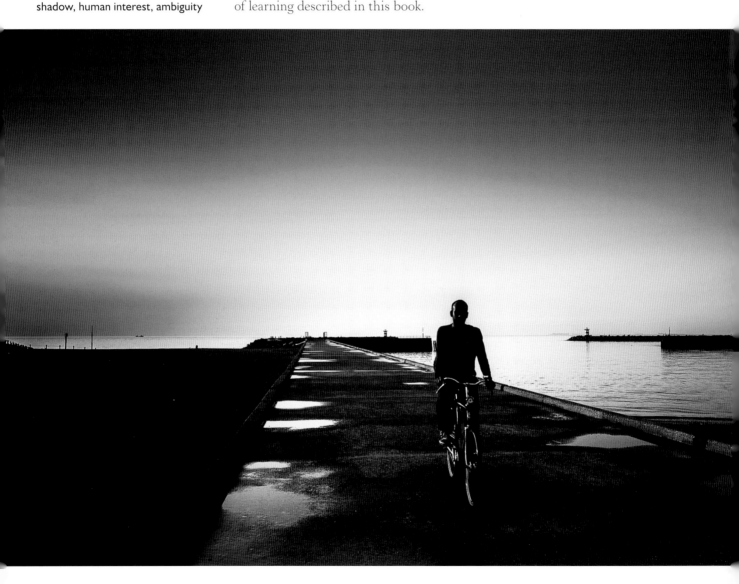

9
GOING FORWARD

In this conclusion to our photographic journey we reflect upon the combination of all human skill into the process of image making. We consider the power of the human mind and our ability to see and communicate what is significant, good and true to us through our photography.

Our journey, if faithfully followed, should lead to two outcomes: a very dog-eared and well- thumbed copy of this book and your having achieved a level of skill in photography you would not have thought possible. Have you looked at the ten images you put away in a special folder or reference collection right at the start of our journey together? If not, now is the moment. I am sure you will see a fundamental change.

As noted right at the beginning, this book is primarily about the capture of the moment. As you have discovered, it is not just about 'camera work' – it is about capturing the shots that, when faithfully processed, will deliver images of outstanding impact. To achieve that we have not concentrated on the technical stuff – there is a list of excellent books covering the technicalities in the bibliography. We have concentrated instead on how you learn the art of great photography through the process of 'burning in' the skills into your non-conscious functioning mind. To do this we have employed an insight from psychology: the more emotionally engaged you are, the more potent the learning process becomes.

We have also employed another great psychological insight: intuition and intuitive judgement can be multi-channelled. The limit of that is ten different schemata or 'bundles' of knowledge and various skills, which in combination summarize what is needed to capture great images. The list we have developed has a wide range of acceptability (at least in the terms used) across national and international photographic authorities as well as practising photographers. Different organizations or individuals might mean slightly different things by each – that's fine: it is how you understood and use the that matters.

However, where this approach changes the game is in the learning approach adopted. To summarize it is as follows:

Break your learning down into the ten skill sets we suggest, practise each one at a time.

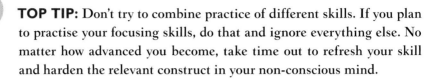

TOP TIP: Don't try to combine practice of different skills. If you plan to practise your focusing skills, do that and ignore everything else. No matter how advanced you become, take time out to refresh your skill and harden the relevant construct in your non-conscious mind.

When practising, choose exercises that take you to the limit of what you can achieve in each of the ten skill sets. Ideally, about an 80% chance of success is recommended. This is deep practice.

Before you start your practice do try to bring yourself to the moment by simple meditative techniques or just listening to music.

As you commence practice, engage your emotions by choosing appropriate music for the theme you are planning to shoot. If you need to feel anger we don't advise picking a fight with your nearest and dearest. Find some music that has the same effect!

Practise the skill set with determination and commitment. We would recommend 10 minutes of practice, 5 minutes rest.

Chimp during the 5-minute resting period. Check for accomplishment of what you were trying to achieve, discard all other criteria.

Make a note in your journal of principal shooting conditions and of any cues that could be relevant in building emotional intensity.

When you get home put your images through raw conversion and then start the post-processing in the way described in Chapter 8. Remember to keep your journal up to date with your best images – scrutinize each image from the perspective of your photographic intent using the ten constructs as a guide to how to bring each image to its peak impact.

Use other techniques to seed your creativity and storytelling powers. Embed them into (4) and (5) above.

Don't forget to emulate the work of great photographers – try to see the world through their eyes. It isn't possible, of course, to directly replicate another photographer's work. You can work from the same location and the same perspective but you will never capture the image the way they have done. The benefit comes from trying to do so – the harder you try with this form of deep practice the more you understand the challenges they faced and how they overcame them. Have a look back at Chapter 7 for our comments on *'using the work of other photographers as a spring board to the future'* to quote the photographer Ralph Gibson.

When trying to capture the essence of other photographers' achievement, do as much research as you can into what inspired them. To successfully pay homage or to mimic a particular style you need to understand their way of looking and seeing and the emotional cues behind their work. What is it your chosen photographer wants to communicate to the viewer and more importantly why? To be good at 'stealing' from other photographers you have to be able to get under their skin and work out how and why they think the way they do.

After a shoot, sort through your images identifying those that you believe have fulfilled your photographic intent. These are your candidate images.

Proceed through pre-processing checking white balance, dynamic range, contrast and any other global adjustments that appear necessary. Check and control for noise. Apply initial pre-sharpening.

TOP TIP: If your image management and processing software allows it, make a number of virtual copies (I suggest three at least) once you have completed the pre-processing stage on your raw images. These virtual copies will allow you to experiment with different post-processing approaches and techniques.

Select a candidate image and put on the music that surrounded its capture. Put the image on full-screen and concentrate on the message it is delivering to you. Look in your journal at the cues you identified at the point of capture and think about them in the context of your image. Note the cues and how you intend to strengthen them. By this point in the learning process we suggest you follow the idea that technique, be it camera or post-processing, is a servant of your vision and intent.

Adjust the crop of the image to optimize its composition and correct any misalignment of horizon or verticals. If there is a problem of converging verticals correct them at this point.

Work on the image, further adjusting its exposure and contrast to suit the mood you are trying to invoke; similarly, emphasize and correct colour balance and saturation or tonality to the same end.

Use selective adjustments to emphasize the cues you see as important and to 'knock back' those you don't. Important tools here are selective exposure, sharpening, clarity, saturation and vibrance. Be careful: it is easy to overdo these adjustments – particularly saturation, clarity and sharpening. They can ruin an image as easily as they can enhance it. Check each adjustment carefully using the full-screen mode on your software (the F key in Lightroom).

ENDNOTE

As we draw this book to a close reflect for a moment on where you started and where you are now and summarize the burning question that has motivated this book: what makes the master photographer?

Our aim has been to give you a route to mastery of your chosen photographic genre. We have introduced you to the simple processes that you can use to build your ability through all the levels of generating great images. Indeed, master photographers produce outstanding images in any genre that stand the test of time. They use their medium in unimagined ways. They produce images like no one else's. They produce a unique tone and vision in their work, they push boundaries and they extend, through their art, the values of our global civilization in many different ways.

There are many differing views as to the constituent qualities of a master in any field. I believe that commitment, passion for your art, persistence in the face of failure, a willingness to engage in deep learning and the ability to accept and profit from criticism are all necessary qualities to embrace. We hope that as this book draws to a close my route to success has worked for you and that those essential qualities are now present in abundance in your photography.

**The House in The Cuillins, Skye
– Alison Price, 2016**

APPENDIX

I

AM I READY? CHECKLIST

AM I READY? CHECKLIST
(basic camera competency)

Can I alter the recording format of my camera (raw, JPEG)?

Can I vary the ISO successfully and set auto-ISO as necessary?

Can I switch modes – programme to aperture priority to shutter priority to manual?

Can I change shooting mode: single shot, continuous low, continuous high?

Can I change the autofocus (AF) modes?

Can I alter exposure metering mode – spot, centre-weighted, matrix?

Can I vary the exposure compensation?

Can I set the rear camera display to show the histogram and out-of-range image areas?

Can I focus an image both manually and automatically?

Do I know how to spot off the brightest part of the image?

Do I know how aperture, shutter speed and ISO are linked to exposure?

Do I know how depth of field varies with exposure and with focal length of lens?

Can I activate the depth of field indicator on my camera?

Do I know how to set the focal length of my camera to a specific distance?

Do I know how to use back button focusing and exposure lock?

APPENDIX
2

PHOTOGRAPHIC ANALYSIS FOR CHAPTER 4, EXERCISE 4.1

PHOTOGRAPHIC ANALYSIS SHEET

Score Each Photograph	Focus	Exposure	Technical	Depth of field	Use of light	Composition	Use of colour or tonality	Narrative	Creativity	Impact
1										
2										
3										
4										
5										
6										
7										
8										
9										
10										
11										
12										

BIBLIOGRAPHY

Harold Davis, *Creative Black and White*. Indianapolis, Indiana: Wiley, 2010.

A good and comprehensive guide to black and white photography with an emphasis on Photoshop processing. Look for the latest edition.

Jerod Foster, *Color: A Photographer's Guide to Directing the Eye, Creating Visual Depth and Conveying Emotion*. San Francisco: Peachpit Press, 2014.

A brilliant book covering all aspects of colour in photography. A perfect addition to Chapter 6.

Freeman Patterson, *Photography and the Art of Seeing: A Visual Perception Workshop*. Richmond Hill, Ontario: Firefly Books, 2012.

Another inspirational teacher who, in some respects, comes closest to our position in this book. Freeman's book is a great follow on to our work on impact in Chapter 8.

Bryan Peterson, *Learning to See Creatively*. New York: Amphoto Books, 2003.

Bryan's book is a joy to read and work with. Although not grasping the nettle of how to systematically build expertise, this lovely book is really inspiring and helpful.

Bryan Peterson, *Understanding Exposure*. New York: Amphoto Books, 2004.

A tour de force around the topic of exposure and the use of light. The explanations are beautifully clear; only the learning method lacks the structure and coherence of this book.

Steve Simon, *The Passionate Photographer*. Berkeley, California: New Riders Press, 2012.

A super book looking at different ways to enhance your photography merging into developing life skills. Not as focused as this book and not offering a rigorous programme for development. But excellent and a great read.

Sebastiao Salgado, *Genesis*, Los Angeles: Taschen, 2013.

This project was Salgado's love letter to the planet. Salgado's work is an inspiration for any photographer. It's a big book but stuffed full of images to learn from.

Peter Stepan (ed.), *Photos that Changed the World*, New York: Prestel Press, 2006.

Here you will find the high impact images that had such a huge impact upon the 20th century. If you are interested in the history of photography and the issues of narrative and impact this book is for you.

Chris Weston, *A Photographic Guide to Exposure*. Lewes, UK: PIP, 2004.

It's a bit dated now but still an excellent book to get off the shelf. Chris is also one of the very best wildlife photographers.

Art Wolfe, *The New Art of Photographing Nature*. New York: Amphoto Books, 2012.

This is a wonderful book by one of the greatest living photographers. In it he and a picture editor critique his images. Truly fabulous and very inspiring.

Art Wolfe, *The Art of the Photograph: Essential Habits for Stronger Compositions*. New York: Amphoto Books, 2013.

This is the perfect reading for Chapter 6 on composition. Art will leave you gasping with the breadth of his insights.

INDEX